The Poems

of

Robert Browning

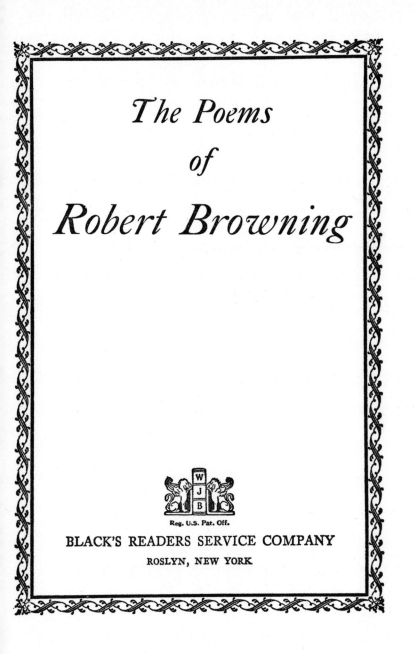

Reg. U.S. Pat. Off.

BLACK'S READERS SERVICE COMPANY

ROSLYN, NEW YORK

CONTENTS

CONTENTS

INTRODUCTION

It would be easy to fill several introductions as long as the present one with what might be called the bare vital statistics of Browning's career; with the major events of his long and full and famous, yet reticently private, life, and with the mere titles and publication dates of his many books. Certain facts, of course, must be given. It is desirable for readers to know that the poet sprang from the loins of the solid British middle class, at Camberwell on May 7, 1812; that his early schooling was marked by a precocity which is often absent from the youth of genius, and his education at home by an amazing irregularity which led him into those "holes and corners of history" which were to furnish his poetry with so many unfamiliar and puzzling allusions; that he attended University College as "a bright handsome youth with long black hair falling over his shoulders"; that he met Miss Elizabeth Barrett in May, 1845, wooed her in one of the most impetuous and celebrated of courtships, raised her from an invalid's couch, married her secretly, and carried her away from the gloomy house in Wimpole Street, far away to the Italian sunshine, in 1846; that he enjoyed fifteen years of married happiness, during which time a son was born to him in 1849; that death robbed him of Elizabeth in 1861, and that thereafter he continued to write more vigorously than ever, pouring out an increasing flood of volumes until, full of years and honors, he died at Venice on December 12, 1889. It may also be desirable for readers to know the sequence of his writings: "Pauline," 1833; "Paracelsus," 1835; "Sordello," 1840; "Pippa Passes," 1841; "Dramatic Lyrics," 1842; "The Return of the Druses," 1843; "The Ring and the Book," 1868—and so on, and on.

But it seems best to devote such space as is available here to Browning's character and the essential nature of the poetry which this volume holds. His wittiest and one of his most understanding biographers, G. K. Chesterton, has insisted that "the great central and solid fact" regarding Robert Browning is that he "was a thoroughly typical Englishman of the middle class." Obviously this statement could be all true only if the typical middle class Englishman were in the habit of writing great poetry, which God and Mr. Chesterton know he is not; but there is more truth in it than at first appears. The central and solid fact regarding Browning is that he was a great and unique poet; the secondary fact is that through his highly individual, even eccentric, poetry he spoke for a class that is infrequently capable of speaking for itself. The philosophy which sustained Browning and inspired his writing was the philosophy which, consciously or unconsciously, sustains though seldom inspires the average millions of the world through the routine of their daily existence. The bored aristocrat, or the bitter Bohemian, or the relentlessly logical philosopher, may sneer at life as a fool's business; but the average man proceeds, and must proceed, upon the assumption that life is worth living from one working day to the next, that the game, despite its ugliness, bewildering turns, injustices, and disappointments, is ultimately worth the candle. Without that faith, blind though it may be, life would cease; and to that faith Robert Browning gave poetic and heroic utterance.

He believed in man, in nature, and in God; he found in imperfection a promise of perfection, and in mortal life a promise of immortality. Always a yea-sayer, he voiced his courageous affirmation as early as "Pauline"—

> Sun-treader, I believe in God, and truth,
> And love. . . .
>
> Know my last state is happy—free from doubt,
> Or touch of fear. Love me and wish me well.

And later, in "Paracelsus"—

> If I stoop
> Into a dark tremendous sea of cloud,
> It is but for a time; I press God's lamp
> Close to my breast; its splendour, soon or late,
> Will pierce the gloom: I shall emerge one day.

Quotations might be added by the score, but the poems themselves lie before us, sounding their dauntless affirmation to all
who will listen. Where Browning believed, he loved—nature,
mankind, and God; and he was a happy lover, for he refused
to admit that the objects of his affection could finally betray
him. Disillusion was impossible for this man who saw "a good
in evil" and who knew that "even hate is but a mask of
Love's"; despair was alien to one who had only to encounter
evil to understand it and explain it in terms of virtue; defeat
could not overwhelm the poet who declared, "I was ever a
fighter."

No one need be told that Browning's kind of heroic optimism
has lately been out of fashion. The nay-sayers have been having their day and making the most of it; but fashion is by its
very definition transitory, and negation, which denies even itself, must lead straight to a suicide's end. Man cannot hope to
outlive his faith in life, and so long as that faith endures
Robert Browning's poems will speak to ears that are not deaf.
And, be sure, they will speak as poetry of a high order.
Thanks to the death of another fashion, the Browning Societies
have ceased to spread their blight over the work of the man
they sought to honor. "I am very far from being a Brown-
ingite," said the author of "The Ring and the Book," and so,
praise be, are most of us to-day. No longer do we look upon
him as a high priest of sacred mysteries or as a designer of
verbal mazes, but as what he really was: a romantic poet who
served his art with an unwavering devotion, whose apparent
eccentricities were the vital stuff of a singularly powerful poetic
personality. Opinions may differ as to what a poet deserves
of the world, but surely the least he deserves is that he should
be read as a poet and as nothing else. That is what the
Browning Societies perversely refused to do for Robert Browning; that is what we can do, and all we can do, for one who
has done so much for us.

BEN RAY REDMAN.

POEMS

POEMS

PROLOGUES

FIFINE AT THE FAIR

THE fancy I had to-day,
  Fancy which turned a fear!
I swam far out in the bay,
  Since waves laughed warm and clear.

I lay and looked at the sun,
  The noon-sun looked at me:
Between us two, no one
  Live creature, that I could see.

Yes! There came floating by
  Me, who lay floating too,
Such a strange butterfly!
  Creature as dear as new:

Because the membraned wings
  So wonderful, so wide,
So sun-suffused, were things
  Like soul and naught beside.

1

A handbreadth overhead!
　　All of the sea my own,
It owned the sky instead;
　　Both of us were alone.

I never shall join its flight,
　　For, naught buoys flesh in air.
If it touch the sea—good night!
　　Death sure and swift waits there.

Can the insect feel the better
　　For watching the uncouth play
Of limbs that slip the fetter,
　　Pretend as they were not clay?

Undoubtedly I rejoice
　　That the air comports so well
With a creature which had the choice
　　Of the land once. Who can tell?

What if a certain soul
　　Which early slipped its sheath,
And has for its home the whole
　　Of heaven, thus look beneath.

Thus watch one who, in the world,
　　Both lives and likes life's way,

Nor wishes the wings unfurled
  That sleep in the worm, they say?

But sometimes when the weather
  Is blue, and warm waves tempt
To free one's self of tether,
  And try a life exempt

From worldly noise and dust,
  In the sphere which overbrims
With passion and thought,—why, just
  Unable to fly, one swims!

By passion and thought upborne,
  One smiles to one's self—"They fare
Scarce better, they need not scorn
  Our sea, who live in the air!"

Emancipate through passion
  And thought, with sea for sky,
We substitute, in a fashion,
  For heaven—poetry:

Which sea, to all intent,
  Gives flesh such noon-disport
As a finer element
  Affords the spirit-sort.

LA SAISIAZ

Whatever they are, we seem.
  Imagine the thing they know;
All deeds they do, we dream;
  Can heaven be else but so?

And meantime, yonder streak
  Meets the horizon's verge;
That is the land, to seek
  If we tire or dread the surge:

Land the solid and safe—
  To welcome again (confess!)
When, high and dry, we chafe
  The body, and don the dress.

Does she look, pity, wonder
  At one who mimics flight,
Swims—heaven above, sea under,
  Yet always earth in sight?

LA SAISIAZ

  Good, to forgive:
    Best, to forget!
    Living, we fret;
  Dying, we live.

Fretless and free,
 Soul, clap thy pinion!
 Earth have dominion,
Body, o'er thee!

Wander at will,
 Day after day,—
 Wander away,
Wandering still—
Soul that canst soar!
 Body may slumber:
 Body shall cumber
Soul-flight no more.

Waft of soul's wing!
 What lies above?
 Sunshine and Love,
Skyblue and Spring!
Body hides—where?
 Ferns of all feather,
 Mosses and heather,
Yours be the care!

TWO POETS OF CROISIC

Such a starved bank of moss
 Till, that May-morn,
Blue ran the flash across:
 Violets were born!

Sky—what a scowl of cloud
  Till, near and far,
Ray on ray split the shroud:
  Splendid, a star!

World—how it walled about
  Life with disgrace
Till God's own smile came out:
  That was thy face!

———

PACCHIAROTTO

Oʜ, the old wall here! How I could pass
  Life in a long midsummer day,
My feet confined to a plot of grass,
  My eyes from a wall not once away!

And lush and lithe do the creepers clothe
  Yon wall I watch, with a wealth of green:
Its bald red bricks draped, nothing loth,
  In lappets of tangle they laugh between.

Now, what is it makes pulsate the robe?
  Why tremble the sprays? What life o'erbrims
The body,—the house, no eye can probe,—
  Divined as, beneath a robe, the limbs?

And there again! But my heart may guess
   Who tripped behind; and she sang perhaps:
So, the old wall throbbed, and its life's excess
   Died out and away in the leafy wraps!

Wall upon wall are between us: life
   And song should away from heart to heart!
I—prison-bird, with a ruddy strife
   At breast, and a lip whence storm-notes start—

Hold on, hope hard in the subtle thing
   That's spirit: though cloistered fast, soar free;
Account as wood, brick, stone, this ring
   Of the rueful neighbors, and—forth to thee!

JOCOSERIA

WANTING is—what?
Summer redundant,
Blueness abundant,
—Where is the blot?
Beamy the world, yet a blank all the same,
—Framework which waits for a picture to frame:
What of the leafage, what of the flower?
Roses embowering with naught they embower!
Come then, complete incompletion, O comer,
Pant through the blueness, perfect the summer!

Breathe but one breath
Rose-beauty above,
And all that was death
Grows life, grows love,
Grows love!

TO ELIZABETH BARRETT BROWNING

MY STAR

ALL that I know
    Of a certain star
Is, it can throw
    (Like the angled spar)
Now a dart of red,
    Now a dart of blue;
Till my friends have said
    They would fain see, too,
My star that dartles the red and the blue!
Then it stops like a bird; like a flower, hangs furled:
    They must solace themselves with the Saturn above
        it.
What matter to me if their star is a world?
    Mine has opened its soul to me; therefore I love it.

ONE WORD MORE

THERE they are, my fifty men and women
Naming me the fifty poems finished!
Take them, Love, the book and me together:
Where the heart lies, let the brain lie also.

Rafael made a century of sonnets,
Made and wrote them in a certain volume
Dinted with the silver-pointed pencil
Else he only used to draw Madonnas:
These, the world might view—but one, the volume.
Who that one, you ask? Your heart instructs you.
Did she live and love it all her lifetime?
Did she drop, his lady of the sonnets,
Die, and let it drop beside her pillow
Where it lay in place of Rafael's glory,
Rafael's cheek so duteous and so loving—
Cheek, the world was wont to hail a painter's,
Rafael's cheek, her love had turned a poet's?

You and I would rather read that volume,
(Taken to his beating bosom by it)
Lean and list the bosom-beats of Rafael,
Would we not? than wonder at Madonnas—
Her, San Sisto names, and Her, Foligno,
Her, that visits Florence in a vision,
Her, that's left with lilies in the Louvre—
Seen by us and all the world in circle.

You and I will never read that volume.
Guido Reni, like his own eye's apple
Guarded long the treasure-book and loved it.

Guido Reni dying, all Bologna
Cried, and the world cried too, "Ours, the treasure!"
Suddenly, as rare things will, it vanished.

Dante once prepared to paint an angel:
Whom to please? You whisper "Beatrice."
While he mused and traced it and retraced it,
(Peradventure with a pen corrodèd
Still by drops of that hot ink he dipped for,
When, his left-hand i' the hair o' the wicked,
Back he held the brow and pricked its stigma,
Bit into the live man's flesh for parchment,
Loosed him, laughed to see the writing rankle,
Let the wretch go festering through Florence)—
Dante, who loved well because he hated,
Hated wickedness that hinders loving,
Dante standing, studying his angel,—
In there broke the folk of his Inferno.
Says he—"Certain people of importance"
(Such he gave his daily dreadful line to)
"Entered and would seize, forsooth, the poet."
Says the poet—"Then I stopped my painting."

You and I would rather see that angel,
Painted by the tenderness of Dante,
Would we not?—than read a fresh Inferno.

You and I will never see that picture.
While he mused on love and Beatrice,
While he softened o'er his outlined angel,
In they broke, those "people of importance:"
We and Bice bear the loss forever.

What of Rafael's sonnets, Dante's picture?
This: no artist lives and loves, that longs not
Once, and only once, and for one only,
(Ah, the prize!) to find his love a language
Fit and fair and simple and sufficient—
Using nature that's an art to others,
Not, this one time, art that's turned his nature.
Ay, of all the artists living, loving,
None but would forego his proper dowry,—
Does he paint? he fain would write a poem,—
Does he write? he fain would paint a picture,
Put to proof art alien to the artist's,
Once, and only once, and for one only,
So to be the man and leave the artist,
Gain the man's joy, miss the artist's sorrow.

Wherefore? Heaven's gift takes earth's abatement!
He who smites the rock and spreads the water,
Bidding drink and live a crowd beneath him,
Even he, the minute makes immortal,
Proves, perchance, but mortal in the minute,
Desecrates, belike, the deed in doing.

While he smites, how can he but remember,
So he smote before, in such a peril,
When they stood and mocked—"Shall smiting help
    us?"
When they drank and sneered—"A stroke is easy!"
When they wiped their mouths and went their journey,
Throwing him for thanks—"But drought was pleas-
    ant."
Thus old memories mar the actual triumph;
Thus the doing savors of disrelish;
Thus achievement lacks a gracious somewhat;
O'er-importuned brows becloud the mandate,
Carelessness or consciousness—the gesture.
For he bears an ancient wrong about him,
Sees and knows again those phalanxed faces,
Hears, yet one time more, the 'customed prelude—
"How shouldst thou, of all men, smite, and save us?"
Guesses what is like to prove the sequel—
"Egypt's flesh-pots—nay, the drought was better."

Oh, the crowd must have emphatic warrant!
Theirs, the Sinai-forehead's cloven brilliance,
Right-arm's rod-sweep, tongue's imperial fiat.
Never dares the man put off the prophet.

Did he love one face from out the thousands,
(Were she Jethro's daughter, white and wifely,
Were she but the Æthiopian bondslave,)

He would envy yon dumb patient camel,
Keeping a reserve of scanty water
Meant to save his own life in the desert;
Ready in the desert to deliver
(Kneeling down to let his breast be opened)
Hoard and life together for his mistress.

I shall never, in the year remaining,
Paint you pictures, no, nor carve you statues,
Make you music that should all-express me;
So it seems: I stand on my attainment.
This of verse alone, one life allows me;
Verse and nothing else have I to give you.
Other heights in other lives, God willing:
All the gifts from all the heights, your own, Love!

Yet a semblance of resource avails us—
Shade so finely touched, love's sense must seize it.
Take these lines, look lovingly and nearly,
Lines I write the first time and the last time.
He who works in fresco, steals a hair-brush,
Curbs the liberal hand, subservient proudly,
Cramps his spirit, crowds its all in little,
Makes a strange art of an art familiar,
Fills his lady's missal-marge with flowerets.
He who blows through bronze, may breathe through
        silver,

Fitly serenade a slumbrous princess.
He who writes, may write for once as I do.

Love, you saw me gather men and women,
Live or dead or fashioned by my fancy,
Enter each and all, and use their service,
Speak from every mouth,—the speech, a poem.
Hardly shall I tell my joys and sorrows,
Hopes and fears, belief and disbelieving:
I am mine and yours—the rest be all men's,
Karshish, Cleon, Norbert, and the fifty.
Let me speak this once in my true person,
Not as Lippo, Roland, or Andrea,
Though the fruit of speech be just this sentence:
Pray you, look on these my men and women,
Take and keep my fifty poems finished;
Where my heart lies, let my brain lie also!
Poor the speech; be how I speak, for all things.

Not but that you know me! Lo, the moon's self!
Here in London, yonder late in Florence,
Still we find her face, the thrice-transfigured.
Curving on a sky imbrued with color,
Drifted over Fiesole by twilight,
Came she, our new crescent of a hair's-breadth.
Full she flared it, lamping Samminiato,
Rounder 'twixt the cypresses and rounder,

Perfect till the nightingales applauded.
Now, a piece of her old self, impoverished,
Hard to greet, she traverses the house-roofs,
Hurries with unhandsome thrift of silver,
Goes dispiritedly, glad to finish.

What, there's nothing in the moon noteworthy?
Nay: for if that moon could love a mortal,
Use, to charm him (so to fit a fancy),
All her magic ('t is the old sweet mythos),
She would turn a new side to her mortal,
Side unseen of herdsman, huntsman, steersman—
Blank to Zoroaster on his terrace,
Blind to Galileo on his turret,
Dumb to Homer, dumb to Keats—him, even!
Think, the wonder of the moonstruck mortal—
When she turns round, comes again in heaven,
Opens out anew for worse or better!
Proves she like some portent of an iceberg
Swimming full upon the ship it founders,
Hungry with huge teeth of splintered crystals?
Proves she as the paved work of a sapphire
Seen by Moses when he climbed the mountain?
Moses, Aaron, Nadab and Abihu
Climbed and saw the very God, the Highest,
Stand upon the paved work of a sapphire.
Like the bodied heaven in his clearness

Shone the stone, the sapphire of that paved work,
When they ate and drank and saw God also!

What were seen? None knows, none ever shall know,
Only this is sure—the sight were other,
Not the moon's same side, born late in Florence
Dying now impoverished here in London.
God be thanked, the meanest of his creatures
Boasts two soul-sides, one to face the world with,
One to show a woman when he loves her!

This I say of me, but think of you, Love!
This to you—yourself my moon of poets!
Ah, but that's the world's side, there's the wonder,
Thus they see you, praise you, think they know you!
There, in turn I stand with them and praise you—
Out of my own self, I dare to phrase it.
But the best is when I glide from out them,
Cross a step or two of dubious twilight,
Come out on the other side, the novel
Silent silver lights and darks undreamed of,
Where I hush and bless myself with silence.

Oh, their Rafael of the dear Madonnas,
Oh, their Dante of the dread Inferno,
Wrote one song—and in my brain I sing it,
Drew one angel—borne, see, on my bosom!

PROSPICE

FEAR death?—to feel the fog in my throat,
  The mist in my face,
When the snows begin, and the blasts denote
  I am nearing the place,
The power of the night, the press of the storm,
  The post of the foe;
Where he stands, the Arch Fear in a visible form,
  Yet the strong man must go:
For the journey is done and the summit attained,
  And the barriers fall,
Though a battle's to fight ere the guerdon be gained,
  The reward of it all.
I was ever a fighter, so—one fight more,
  The best and the last!
I would hate that death bandaged my eyes, and
    forbore,
  And bade me creep past.
No! let me taste the whole of it, fare like my peers
  The heroes of old,
Bear the brunt, in a minute pay glad life's arrears
  Of pain, darkness and cold.
For sudden the worst turns the best to the brave,
  The black minute's at end,
And the elements' rage, the fiend-voices that rave,
  Shall dwindle, shall blend,

Shall change, shall become first a peace out of pain,
  Then a light, then thy breast,
O thou soul of my soul! I shall clasp thee again,
  And with God be the rest!

SONGS

FERISHTAH'S FANCIES

Round us the wild creatures, overhead the trees,
Underfoot the moss-tracks,—life and love with these!
I to wear a fawn-skin, thou to dress in flowers:
All the long lone summer-day, that greenwood life of
    ours!

Rich-pavilioned, rather,—still the world without,—
Inside—gold-roofed silk-walled silence round about!
Queen it thou on purple,—I, at watch, and ward
Couched beneath the columns, gaze, thy slave, love's
    guard!

So, for us no world? Let throngs press thee to me!
Up and down amid men, heart by heart fare we!
Welcome squalid vesture, harsh voice, hateful face!
God is soul, souls I and thou: with souls should souls
    have place.

Wish no word unspoken, want no look away!
What if words were but mistake, and looks—too sud-
    den, say!
Be unjust for once, Love! Bear it—well I may!

Do me justice always? Bid my heart—their shrine—
Render back its store of gifts, old looks and words of
thine
—Oh, so all unjust—the less deserved, the more
divine?

You groped your way across my room i' the drear
dark dead of night;
At each fresh step a stumble was: but, once your lamp
alight,
Easy and plain you walked again: so soon all wrong
grew right!

What lay on floor to trip your foot? Each object, late
awry,
Looked fitly placed, nor proved offence to footing free
—for why?
The lamp showed all, discordant late, grown simple
symmetry.

Be love your light and trust your guide, with these
explore my heart!
No obstacle to trip you then, strike hands and souls
apart!
Since rooms and hearts are furnished so,—light shows
you,—needs love start?

Man I am and man would be, Love—merest man and
  nothing more.
Bid me seem no other! Eagles boast of pinions—let
  them soar!
I may put forth angel's plumage, once unmanned, but
  not before.

Now on earth, to stand suffices,—nay, if kneeling
  serves, to kneel:
Here you front me, here I find the all of heaven that
  earth can feel:
Sense looks straight,—not over, under,—perfect sees
  beyond appeal.

Good you are and wise, full circle: what to me were
  more outside?
Wiser wisdom, better goodness? Ah, such want the
  angel's wide
Sense to take and hold and keep them! Mine at least
  has never tried.

Fire is in the flint: true, once a spark escapes,
Fire forgets the kinship, soars till fancy shapes
Some befitting cradle where the babe had birth—
Wholly heaven's the product, unallied to earth.
Splendors recognized as perfect in the star!—
In our flint their home was, housed as now they are.

So, the head aches and the limbs are faint!
　Flesh is a burden—even to you!
Can I force a smile with a fancy quaint?
　Why are my ailments none or few?

In the soul of me sits sluggishness:
　Body so strong and will so weak:
The slave stands fit for the labor—yes,
　But the master's mandate is still to seek.

You, now—what if the outside clay
　Helped, not hindered the inside flame?
My dim to-morrow—your plain to-day,
　Yours the achievement, mine the aim?

So were it rightly, so shall it be!
　Only, while earth we pace together
For the purpose apportioned you and me,
　Closer we tread for a common tether.

You shall sigh, "Wait for his sluggish soul!
　Shame he should lag, not lamed as I!"
May not I smile, "Ungained her goal:
　Body may reach her—by and by"?

When I vexed you and you chid me,
　And I owned my fault and turned
My cheek the way you bid me,
　And confessed the blow well earned,—

My comfort all the while was
  —Fault was faulty—near, not quite!
Do you wonder why the smile was?
  O'erpunished wrong grew right.

But faults, you ne'er suspected,
  Nay, praised, no faults at all,—
Those would you had detected—
  Crushed eggs whence snakes could crawl!

Once I saw a chemist take a pinch of powder
—Simple dust it seemed—and half-unstop a phial:
—Out dropped harmless dew. "Mixed nothings make"
      (quoth he)
"Something!" So they did: a thunderclap, but
      louder—
Lightning-flash, but fiercer—put spectators' nerves to
      trial:
Sure enough, we learned what was, imagined what
      might be.

Had I no experience how a lip's mere tremble,
Look's half hesitation, cheek's just change of color,
These effect a heartquake,—how should I conceive
What a heaven there may be? Let it but resemble
Earth myself have known! No bliss that's finer,
      fuller,

Only—bliss that lasts, they say, and fain would I
    believe.

Verse-making was least of my virtues: I viewed with
    despair
Wealth that never yet was but might be—all that
    verse-making were
If the life would but lengthen to wish, let the mind be
    laid bare.
So I said "To do little is bad, to do nothing is
    worse"—
       And made verse.

Love-making—how simple a matter! No depths to
    explore,
No heights in a life to ascend! No disheartening
    Before,
No affrighting Hereafter,—love now will be love
    evermore.
So I felt "To keep silence were folly:"—all language
    above,
       I made love.

Not with my Soul, Love!—bid no soul like mine
  Lap thee around nor leave the poor Sense room!
Soul,—travel-worn, toil-weary,—would confine
  Along with Soul, Soul's gains from glow and gloom,

Captures from soarings high and divings deep.
Spoil-laden Soul, how should such memories sleep?
  Take Sense, too—let me love entire and whole—
    Not with my Soul!

Eyes shall meet eyes and find no eyes between,
  Lips feed on lips, no other lips to fear!
No past, no future—so thine arms but screen
  The present from surprise! not there, 't is here—
Not then, 't is now:—back, memories that intrude!
Make, Love, the universe our solitude,
  And, over all the rest, oblivion roll—
    Sense quenching Soul!

Ask not one least word of praise!
  Words declare your eyes are bright?
What then meant that summer day's
Silence spent in one long gaze?
  Was my silence wrong or right?

Words of praise were all to seek!
  Face of you and form of you,
Did they find the praise so weak
When my lips just touched your cheek—
  Touch which let my soul come through?

"Why from the world," Ferishtah smiled, "should
    thanks

Go to this work of mine? If worthy praise,
Praised let it be and welcome: as verse ranks,
    So rate my verse: if good therein outweighs
    Aught faulty judged, judge justly! Justice **says:**
Be just to fact, or blaming or approving:
But—generous? No, nor loving!

"Loving! what claim to love has work of mine?
    Concede my life were emptied of its gains
To furnish forth and fill work's strict confine,
    Who works so for the world's sake—he complains
    With cause when hate, not love, rewards his pains.
I looked beyond the world for truth and beauty:
Sought, found, and did my duty."

PARACELSUS

I HEAR a voice, perchance I heard
Long ago, but all too low,
So that scarce a care it stirred
If the voice were real or no:
I heard it in my youth when first
The waters of my life outburst:
But, now their stream ebbs faint, I hear
That voice, still low, but fatal-clear—
As if all poets, God ever meant
Should save the world, and therefore lent
Great gifts to, but who, proud, refused

To do his work, or lightly used
Those gifts, or failed through weak endeavor,
So, mourn cast off by him forever,—
As if these leaned in airy ring
To take me; this the song they sing.

"Lost, lost! yet come,
With our wan troop make thy home.
Come, come! for we
Will not breathe, so much as breathe
Reproach to thee,
Knowing what thou sink'st beneath.
So sank we in those old years,
We who bid thee, come! thou last
Who, living yet, hast life o'erpast.
And altogether we, thy peers,
Will pardon crave for thee, the last
Whose trial is done, whose lot is cast
With those who watch but work no more,
Who gaze on life but live no more
Yet we trusted thou shouldst speak
The message which our lips, too weak,
Refused to utter,—shouldst redeem
Our fault: such trust, and all a dream!

Yet we chose thee a birthplace
Where the richness ran to flowers:

Couldst not sing one song for grace?
Not make one blossom man's and ours?
Must one more recreant to his race
Die with unexerted powers,
And join us, leaving as he found
The world, he was to loosen, bound?
Anguish! ever and forever;
Still beginning, ending never!
Yet, lost and last one, come!
How couldst understand, alas,
What our pale ghosts strove to say,
As their shades did glance and pass
Before thee night and day?
Thou wast blind as we were dumb:
Once more, therefore, come, O come!
How should we clothe, how arm the spirit
Shall next thy post of life inherit—
How guard him from thy speedy ruin?
Tell us of thy sad undoing
Here, where we sit, ever pursuing
Our weary task, ever renewing
Sharp sorrow, far from God who gave
Our powers, and man they could not save!"

Heap cassia, sandal-buds and stripes
Of labdanum, and aloe-balls,
Smeared with dull nard an Indian wipes

From out her hair: such balsam falls
Down sea-side mountain pedestals,
From tree-tops where tired winds are fain,
Spent with the vast and howling main,
To treasure half their island-gain.

And strew faint sweetness from some old
  Egyptian's fine worm-eaten shroud
Which breaks to dust when once unrolled;
  Or shredded perfume, like a cloud
From closet long to quiet vowed,
With mothed and dropping arras hung,
Mouldering her lute and books among,
As when a queen, long dead, was young.

  Over the sea our galleys went,
With cleaving prows in order brave
To a speeding wind and a bounding wave
  A gallant armament:
Each bark built out of a forest-tree
  Left leafy and rough as first it grew,
And nailed all over the gaping sides,
Within and without, with black bull-hides,
Seethed in fat and suppled in flame,
To bear the playful billows' game:
So, each good ship was rude to see,

Rude and bare to the outward view,
  But each upbore a stately tent
Where cedar pales in scented row
Kept out the flakes of the dancing brine,
And an awning drooped the mast below,
In fold on fold of the purple fine,
That neither noontide nor starshine
Nor moonlight cold which maketh mad,
  Might pierce the regal tenement.
When the sun dawned, oh, gay and glad
We set the sail and plied the oar;
But when the night-wind blew like breath,
For joy of one day's voyage more,
We sang together on the wide sea,
Like men at peace on a peaceful shore:
Each sail was loosed to the wind so free,
Each helm made sure by the twilight star,
And in a sleep as calm as death,
We, the voyagers from afar,
  Lay stretched along, each weary crew
In a circle round its wondrous tent
Whence gleamed soft light and curled rich scent
  And with light and perfume, music too:
So the stars wheeled round, and the darkness past
And at morn we started beside the mast,
And still each ship was sailing fast.

Now, one morn, land appeared—a speck
Dim trembling betwixt sea and sky:
"Avoid it," cried our pilot, "check
   The shout, restrain the eager eye!"
But the heaving sea was black behind
For many a night and many a day,
And land, though but a rock, drew nigh;
So, we broke the cedar pales away,
Let the purple awning flap in the wind,
   And a statue bright was on every deck!
We shouted, every man of us,
And steered right into the harbor thus,
With pomp and pæan glorious.

A hundred shapes of lucid stone!
   All day we built its shrine for each,
A shrine of rock for every one,
Nor paused till in the westering sun
   We sat together on the beach
To sing because our task was done.
When lo! what shouts and merry songs!
What laughter all the distance stirs!
A loaded raft with happy throngs
Of gentle islanders!
"Our isles are just at hand," they cried,
   "Like cloudlets faint in even sleeping.
Our temple-gates are opened wide,

Our olive-groves thick shade are keeping
For these majestic forms"—they cried.
Oh, then we awoke with sudden start
From our deep dream, and knew, too late,
How bare the rock, how desolate.
Which had received our precious freight:
 Yet we called out—"Depart!
Our gifts, once given, must here abide.
 Our work is done; we have no heart
To mar our work,"—we cried.

Thus the Mayne glideth
Where my Love abideth.
Sleep 's no softer: it proceeds
On through lawns, on through meads,
On and on, whate'er befall,
Meandering and musical,
Though the niggard pasturage
Bears not on its shaven ledge
Aught but weeds and waving grasses
To view the river as it passes,
Save here and there a scanty patch
Of primroses too faint to catch
A weary bee.

And scarce it pushes
Its gentle way through strangling rushes
Where the glossy kingfisher

Flutters when noon-heats are near,
Glad the shelving banks to shun,
Red and steaming in the sun,
Where the shrew-mouse with pale throat
Burrows, and the speckled stoat;
Where the quick sandpipers flit
In and out the marl and grit
That seems to breed them, brown as they:
Naught disturbs its quiet way,
Save some lazy stork that springs,
Trailing it with legs and wings,
Whom the shy fox from the hill
Rouses, creep he ne'er so still.

A BLOT IN THE 'SCUTCHEON

THERE'S a woman like a dew-drop, she's so purer than
    the purest;
And her noble heart's the noblest, yes, and her sure
    faith's the surest:
And her eyes are dark and humid, like the depth on
    depth of lustre
Hid i' the harebell, while her tresses, sunnier than the
    wild-grape cluster,
Gush in golden-tinted plenty down her neck's rose-
    misted marble:

Then her voice's music . . . call it the well's bub-
    bling, the bird's warble!

And this woman says, "My days were sunless and
    my nights were moonless,
Parched the pleasant April herbage, and the lark's
    heart's outbreak tuneless,
If you loved me not!" And I who—(ah, for words of
    flame!) adore her,
Who am mad to lay my spirit prostrate palpably be-
    fore her—

I may enter at her portal soon, as now her lattice
    takes me,
And by noontide as by midnight make her mine, as
    hers she makes me!

BALLADS

CAVALIER TUNES

MARCHING ALONG

KENTISH Sir Byng stood for his King,
Bidding the crop-headed Parliament swing:
And, pressing a troop unable to stoop
And see the rogues flourish and honest folk **droop**,
Marched them along, fifty-score strong,
Great-hearted gentlemen, singing this song.

God for King Charles! Pym and such carles
To the Devil that prompts 'em their treasonous **parles!**
Cavaliers, up! Lips from the cup,
Hands from the pasty, nor bite take nor sup
Till you're—
   CHORUS.—Marching along, fifty-score strong,
       Great-hearted gentlemen, singing **this**
       song.

Hampden to hell, and his obsequies' knell.
Serve Hazelrig, Fiennes, and young Harry **as well!**
England, good cheer! Rupert is near!
Kentish and loyalists, keep we not here,

Cho.—Marching along, fifty-score strong,
    Great-hearted gentlemen, singing this song?

Then, God for King Charles! Pym and his snarls
To the Devil that pricks on such pestilent carles!
Hold by the right, you double your might;
So, onward to Nottingham, fresh for the fight,
   Cho.—March we along, fifty-score strong,
    Great-hearted gentlemen, singing this song!

GIVE A ROUSE

King Charles, and who 'll do him right now?
King Charles, and who 's ripe for fight now?
Give a rouse: here 's, in hell's despite now,
King Charles!

Who gave me the goods that went since?
Who raised me the house that sank once?
Who helped me to gold I spent since?
Who found me in wine you drank once?
  Cho.—King Charles, and who 'll do him right now?
    King Charles, and who's ripe for fight now?
    Give a rouse: here 's, in hell's despite now,
    King Charles!

To whom used my boy George quaff else,
By the old fool's side that begot him?

For whom did he cheer and laugh else,
While Noll's damned troopers shot him?
  CHO.—King Charles, and who 'll do him right now?
    King Charles, and who's ripe for fight now?
    Give a rouse: here 's, in hell's despite now
    King Charles!

BOOT AND SADDLE

Boot, saddle, to horse, and away!
Rescue my castle before the hot day
Brightens to blue from its silvery gray.
  CHO.—Boot, saddle, to horse, and away!

Ride past the suburbs, asleep as you'd say;
Many's the friend there, will listen and pray
"God's luck to gallants that strike up the lay—
  CHO.—Boot, saddle, to horse, and away!"

Forty miles off, like a roebuck at bay,
Flouts Castle Brancepeth the Roundheads' array:
Who laughs, "Good fellows ere this, by my fay,
  CHO.—Boot, saddle, to horse, and away!"

Who? My wife Gertrude; that, honest and gay,
Laughs when you talk of surrendering, "Nay!
I've better counsellors; what counsel they?
  CHO.—Boot, saddle, to horse, and away!"

GOOD NEWS FROM GHENT

[16—]

I sprang to the stirrup, and Joris, and he;
I galloped, Dirck galloped, we galloped all three;
"Good speed!" cried the watch, as the gatebolts un-
     drew;
"Speed!" echoed the wall to us galloping through;
Behind shut the postern, the lights sank to rest,
And into the midnight we galloped abreast.

Not a word to each other; we kept the great pace
Neck by neck, stride by stride, never changing our
     place;
I turned in my saddle and made its girths tight,
Then shortened each stirrup, and set the pique right,
Rebuckled the cheek-strap, chained slacker the bit,
Nor galloped less steadily Roland a whit.

'T was moonset at starting; but while we drew near
Lokeren, the cocks crew and twilight dawned clear;
At Boom, a great yellow star came out to see;
At Düffeld, 't was morning as plain as could be;
And from Mecheln church-steeple we heard the half
     chime,
So Joris broke silence with, "Yet there is time!"

At Aershot, up leaped of a sudden the sun,
And against him the cattle stood black every one,
To stare through the mist at us galloping past,
And I saw my stout galloper Roland at last,
With resolute shoulders, each butting away
The haze, as some bluff river headland its spray:

And his low head and crest, just one sharp ear bent
      back
For my voice, and the other pricked out on his track;
And one eye's black intelligence,—ever that glance
O'er its white edge at me, his own master, askance!
And the thick heavy spume-flakes which aye and
      anon
His fierce lips shook upwards in galloping on.

By Hasselt, Dirck groaned; and cried Joris, "Stay
      spur!
Your Roos galloped bravely, the fault 's not in her.
We'll remember at Aix"—for one heard the quick
      wheeze
Of her chest, saw the stretched neck and staggering
      knees,
And sunk tail, and horrible heave of the flank,
As down on her haunches she shuddered and sank.

So, we were left galloping, Joris and I,
Past Looz and past Tongres, no cloud in the sky;

The broad sun above laughed a pitiless laugh,
'Neath our feet broke the brittle bright stubble like
      chaff;
Till over by Dalhem a dome-spire sprang white,
And "Gallop," gasped Joris, "for Aix is in sight!"

"How they'll greet us!"—and all in a moment his roan
Rolled neck and croup over, lay dead as a stone;
And there was my Roland to bear the whole weight
Of the news which alone could save Aix from her fate,
With his nostrils like pits full of blood to the brim,
And with circles of red for his eye-sockets' rim.

Then I cast loose my buffcoat, each holster let fall,
Shook off both my jack-boots, let go belt and all,
Stood up in the stirrup, leaned, patted his ear,
Called my Roland his pet-name, my horse without
      peer;
Clapped my hands, laughed and sang, any noise, bad
      or good,
Till at length into Aix Roland galloped and stood.

And all I remember is—friends flocking round
As I sat with his head 'twixt my knees on the ground;
And no voice but was praising this Roland of mine,
As I poured down his throat our last measure of wine,
Which (the burgesses voted by common consent)
Was no more than his due who brought good news
      from Ghent.

HERVÉ RIEL

On the sea and at the Hogue, sixteen hundred ninety-
    two,
  Did the English fight the French,—woe to France!
And, the thirty-first of May, helter-skelter through
    the blue,
Like a crowd of frightened porpoises a shoal of sharks
    pursue,
  Came crowding ship on ship to Saint Malo on the
    Rance,
With the English fleet in view.

'T was the squadron that escaped, with the victor in
    full chase;
  First and foremost of the drove, in his great ship
    Damfreville;
    Close on him fled, great and small,
    Twenty-two good ships in all;
And they signalled to the place
"Help the winners of a race!
  Get us guidance, give us harbor, take us quick—or
    quicker still,
Here's the English can and will!"

Then the pilots of the place put out brisk and leapt on
    board;

"Why, what hope or chance have ships like these
    to pass?" laughed they:
'Rocks to starboard, rocks to port, all the passage
    scarred and scored,
Shall the 'Formidable' here with her twelve and eighty
    guns
    Think to make the river-mouth by the single nar-
      row way,
Trust to enter where 't is ticklish for a craft of twenty
    tons,
    And with the flow at full beside?
    Now, 't is slackest ebb of tide.
  Reach the mooring? Rather say,
While rocks stands or water runs,
    Not a ship will leave the bay!"

Then was called a council straight.
Brief and bitter the debate:
"Here's the English at our heels; would you have
    them take in tow
All that's left us of the fleet linked together stern
    and bow,
For a prize to Plymouth Sound?
Better run the ships aground!"
  (Ended Damfreville his speech).
"Not a minute more to wait!
  Let the Captains all and each

Shove ashore, then blow up, burn the vessels on the
    beach!
France must undergo her fate.

"Give the word!" But no such word
Was ever spoke or heard;
    For up stood, for out stepped, for in struck amid
        all these
—A Captain? A Lieutenant? A Mate—first, second,
    third?
    No such man of mark, and meet
    With his betters to compete!
    But a simple Breton sailor pressed by Tourville
        for the fleet,
A poor coasting-pilot he, Hervé Riel, the Croisickese.

And "What mockery or malice have we here?" cries
    Hervé Riel:
    "Are you mad, you Malouins? Are you cowards,
        fools, or rogues?
Talk to me of rocks and shoals, me who took the
    soundings, tell
On my fingers every bank, every shallow, every swell
    'Twixt the offing here and Grève where the river
        disembogues?
Are you bought by English gold? Is it love the lying
    's for?
    Morn and eve, night and day,

Have I piloted your bay,
Entered free and anchored fast at the foot of Solidor.
Burn the fleet and ruin France? That were worse
than fifty Hogues!
Sirs, they know I speak the truth! Sirs, believe
me there's a way!
Only let me lead the line,
Have the biggest ship to steer,
Get this 'Formidable' clear,
Make the others follow mine,
And I lead them, most and least, by a passage I know
well,
Right to Solidor past Grève,
And there lay them safe and sound;
And if one ship misbehave,
—Keel so much as grate the ground,
Why, I've nothing but my life,—here's my head!"
cries Hervé Riel.

Not a minute more to wait.
"Steer us in, then, small and great!
Take the helm, lead the line, save the squadron!"
cried its chief.
Captains, give the sailor place!
He is Admiral, in brief.
Still the north-wind, by God's grace!
See the noble fellow's face

As the big ship, with a bound,
Clears the entry like a hound,
Keeps the passage as its inch of way were the wid⌐
    sea's profound!
  See, safe through shoal and rock,
  How they follow in a flock,
Not a ship that misbehaves, not a keel that grates the
    ground,
  Not a spar that comes to grief!
The peril, see, is past,
All are harbored to the last,
And just as Hervé Riel hollas "Anchor!"—sure as
    fate,
Up the English come—too late!

So, the storm subsides to calm:
  They see the green trees wave
  On the heights o'erlooking Grève.
Hearts that bled are stanched with balm.
"Just our rapture to enhance,
  Let the English rake the bay,
Gnash their teeth and glare askance
  As they cannonade away!
'Neath rampired Solidor pleasant riding on the
    Rance!"
How hope succeeds despair on each Captain's counte-
    nance!

Out burst all with one accord,
  "This is Paradise for Hell!
    Let France, let France's King
    Thank the man that did the thing!"
With a shout, and all one word,
  "Hervé Riel!"
As he stepped in front once more,
  Not a symptom of surprise
  In the frank blue Breton eyes,
Just the same man as before.

Then said Damfreville, "My friend,
I must speak out at the end,
  Though I find the speaking hard.
Praise is deeper than the lips:
You have saved the King his ships,
  You must name your own reward.
'Faith, our sun was near eclipse!
Demand whate'er you will,
France remains your debtor still.
Ask to heart's content and have! or my name's not
    Damfreville."

Then a beam of fun outbroke
On the bearded mouth that spoke,
As the honest heart laughed through
Those frank eyes of Breton blue:

"Since I needs must say my say,
   Since on board the duty's done,
      And from Malo Roads to Croisic Point, what is it
         but a run?—
Since 't is ask and have, I may—
   Since the others go ashore—
Come! A good whole holiday!
   Leave to go and see my wife, whom I call the Belle
      Aurore!"
   That he asked and that he got,—nothing more.

Name and deed alike are lost:
Not a pillar nor a post
   In his Croisic keeps alive the feat as it befell;
Not a head in white and black
On a single fishing-smack,
In memory of the man but for whom had gone to
      wrack
   All that France saved from the fight whence Eng-
      land bore the bell.
Go to Paris: rank on rank
   Search the heroes flung pell-mell
On the Louvre, face and flank!
   You shall look long enough ere you come to Hervé
      Riel.
So, for better and for worse,
Hervé Riel, accept my verse!

In my verse, Hervé Riel, do thou once more
Save the squadron, honor France, love thy wife the
  Belle Aurore!

MUCKLE-MOUTH MEG

FROWNED the Laird on the Lord: "So, red-handed I
    catch thee?
  Death-doomed by our Law of the Border!
We've a gallows outside and a chiel to dispatch thee:
  Who trespasses—hangs: all's in order."

He met frown with smile, did the young English
    gallant:
  Then the Laird's dame: "Nay, Husband, I beg!
He's comely: be merciful! Grace for the callant
  —If he marries our Muckle-mouth Meg!"

"No mile-wide-mouthed monster of yours do I marry:
  Grant rather the gallows!" laughed he.
"Foul fare kith and kin of you—why do you tarry?"
  "To tame your fierce temper!" quoth she.

"Shove him quick in the Hole, shut him fast for a
    week:
  Cold, darkness, and hunger work wonders:

Who lion-like roars now, mouse-fashion will squeak,
And 'it rains' soon succeed to 'it thunders.'"

A week did he bide in the cold and the dark
   —Not hunger: for duly at morning
In flitted a lass, and a voice like a lark
   Chirped, "Muckle-mouth Meg still ye're scorning?

"Go hang, but here's parritch to hearten ye first!"
   "Did Meg's muckle-mouth boast within some
Such music as yours, mine should match it or burst:
   No frog-jaws! So tell folk, my Winsome!"

Soon week came to end, and, from Hole's door set
      wide,
   Out he marched, and there waited the lassie:
"Yon gallows, or Muckle-mouth Meg for a bride!
   Consider! Sky's blue and turf's grassy:

"Life's sweet: shall I say ye wed Muckle-mouth
      Meg?"
   "Not I," quoth the stout heart: "too eerie
The mouth that can swallow a bubblyjock's egg;
   Shall I let it munch mine? Never, Dearie!"

"Not Muckle-mouth Meg? Wow, the obstinate man!
   Perhaps he would rather wed me!"
"Ay, would he—with just for a dowry your can!"
   "I'm Muckle-mouth Meg," chirruped she.

"Then so—so—so—so—" as he kissed her apace—
  "Will I widen thee out till thou turnest
From Margaret Minnikin-mou', by God's grace,
  To Muckle-mouth Meg in good earnest!"

MONOLOGUES

SAUL

SAID Abner, "At last thou art come! Ere I tell, ere
    thou speak,
Kiss my cheek, wish me well!" Then I wished it, and
    did kiss his cheek.
And he: "Since the King, O my friend, for thy counte-
    nance sent,
Neither drunken nor eaten have we; nor until from
    his tent
Thou return with the joyful assurance the King liveth
    yet,
Shall our lip with the honey be bright, with the water
    be wet.
For out of the black mid-tent's silence, a space of
    three days,
Not a sound hath escaped to thy servants, of prayer
    nor of praise,
To betoken that Saul and the Spirit have ended their
    strife,
And that, faint in his triumph, the monarch sinks back
    upon life.
Yet now my heart leaps, O beloved! God's child
    with his dew

On thy gracious gold hair, and those lilies still living
    and blue
Just broken to twine round thy harp-strings, as if no
    wild heat
Were now raging to torture the desert!"

                Then I, as was meet,
Knelt down to the God of my fathers, and rose on my
    feet,
And ran o'er the sand burnt to powder. The tent was
    unlooped;
I pulled up the spear that obstructed, and under I
    stooped;
Hands and knees on the slippery grass-patch, all
    withered and gone,
That extends to the second enclosure, I groped my
    way on
Till I felt where the foldskirts fly open. Then once
    more I prayed,
And opened the foldskirts and entered, and was not
    afraid
But spoke, "Here is David, thy servant!" And no
    voice replied.
At the first I saw naught but the blackness: but soon
    I descried
A something more black than the blackness—the vast,
    the upright

Main prop which sustains the pavilion: and slow into
    sight
Grew a figure against it, gigantic and blackest of all.
Then a sunbeam, that burst through the tent-roof,
    showed Saul.

He stood as erect as that tent-prop, both arms
    stretched out wide
On the great cross-support in the centre, that goes to
    each side;
He relaxed not a muscle, but hung there as, caught in
    his pangs
And waiting his change, the king-serpent all heavily
    hangs,
Far away from his kind, in the pine, till deliverance
    come
With the spring-time,—so agonized Saul, drear and
    stark, blind and dumb.

Then I tuned my harp,—took off the lilies we twine
    round its chords
Lest they snap 'neath the stress of the noontide—·
    those sunbeams like swords!
And I first played the tune all our sheep know, as, one
    after one,
So docile they come to the pen-door till folding be
    done.

They are white and untorn by the bushes, for lo, they
    have fed
Where the long grasses stifle the water within the
    stream's bed;
And now one after one seeks its lodging, as star fol-
    lows star
Into eve and the blue far above us,—so blue and so
    far!

—Then the tune for which quails on the corn-land
    will each leave his mate
To fly after the player; then, what makes the crickets
    elate
Till for boldness they fight one another; and then,
    what has weight
To set the quick jerboa a-musing outside his sand
    house—
There are none such as he for a wonder, half bird and
    half mouse!
God made all the creatures and gave them our love
    and our fear,
To give sign, we and they are his children, one family
    here.

Then I played the help-tune of our reapers, their
    wine-song, when hand
Grasps at hand, eye lights eye in good friendship, and
    great hearts expand

And grow one in the sense of this world's life.—-And
      then, the last song

When the dead man is praised on his journey—"Bear,
      bear him along,

With his few faults shut up like dead flowerets! Are
      balm seeds not here

To console us? The land has none left such as he on
      the bier.

Oh, would we might keep thee, my brother!"—And
      then, the glad chaunt

Of the marriage,—first go the young maidens next,
      she whom we vaunt

As the beauty, the pride of our dwelling.—And then,
      the great march

Wherein man runs to man to assist him and buttress
      an arch

Naught can break; who shall harm them, our friends?
      Then, the chorus intoned

As the Levites go up to the altar in glory enthroned.

But I stopped here: for here in the darkness Saul
      groaned.

And I paused, held my breath in such silence, and
      listened apart;

And the tent shook, for mighty Saul shuddered: and
      sparkles 'gan dart

From the jewels that woke in his turban, at once with
    a start,

All its lordly male-sapphires, and rubies courageous
    at heart.

So the head: but the body still moved not, still hung
    there erect.

And I bent once again to my playing, pursued it
    unchecked,

As I sang:—

"Oh, our manhood's prime vigor! No spirit feels
    waste,

Not a muscle is stopped in its playing nor sinew un-
    braced.

Oh, the wild joys of living! the leaping from rock up to
    rock,

The strong rending of boughs from the fir-tree, the
    cool silver shock

Of the plunge in a pool's living water, the hunt of the
    bear,

And the sultriness showing the lion is couched in his
    lair.

And the meal, the rich dates yellowed over with gold
    dust divine,

And the locust-flesh steeped in the pitcher, the full
    draught of wine.

And the sleep in the dried river-channel where bul-
    rushes tell

That the water was wont to go warbling so softly and
    well.

How good is man's life, the mere living! how fit to
    employ

All the heart and the soul and the senses forever in
    joy!

Hast thou loved the white locks of thy father, whose
    sword thou didst guard

When he trusted thee forth with the armies, for glori-
    ous reward?

Didst thou see the thin hands of thy mother held up
    as men sung

The low song of the nearly-departed, and hear her
    faint tongue

Joining in while it could to the witness, 'Let one more
    attest,

I have lived, seen God's hand through a lifetime, and
    all was for best'?

Then they sung through their tears in strong triumph,
    not much, but the rest.

And thy brothers, the help and the contest, the work-
    ing whence grew

Such result as, from seething grape-bundles, the spirit
    strained true:

And the friends of thy boyhood—that boyhood of
wonder and hope,
Present promise and wealth of the future beyond the
eye's scope,—
Till lo, thou art grown to a monarch; a people is
thine;
And all gifts, which the world offers singly, on one
head combine!
On one head, all the beauty and strength, love and
rage (like the throe
That, a-work in the rock, helps its labor and lets the
gold go)
High ambition and deeds which surpass it, fame
crowning them,—all
Brought to blaze on the head of one creature—King
Saul!"

And lo, with that leap of my spirit,—heart, hand,
harp and voice,
Each lifting Saul's name out of sorrow, each bidding
rejoice
Saul's fame in the light it was made for—as when,
dare I say,
The Lord's army, in rapture of service, strains through
its array,
And upsoareth the cherubim-chariot—"Saul!" cried I,
and stopped,

And waited the thing that should follow. Then Saul,
    who hung propped

By the tent's cross-support in the centre, was struck
    by his name.

Have ye seen when Spring's arrowy summons goes
    right to the aim,

And some mountain, the last to withstand her, that
    held (he alone,

While the vale laughed in freedom and flowers) on a
    broad bust of stone

A year's snow bound about for a breastplate,—leaves
    grasp of the sheet?

Fold on fold all at once it crowds thunderously down
    to his feet,

And there fronts you, stark, black, but alive yet, your
    mountain of old,

With his rents, the successive bequeathings of ages
    untold—

Yea, each harm got in fighting your battles, each fur-
    row and scar

Of his head thrust 'twixt you and the tempest—all
    hail, there they are!

—Now again to be softened with verdure, again hold
    the nest

Of the dove, tempt the goat and its young to the green
    on his crest

For their food in the ardors of summer. One long
    shudder thrilled

All the tent till the very air tingled, then sank and
    was stilled

At the King's self left standing before me, released
    and aware.

What was gone, what remained? All to traverse
    'twixt hope and despair,

Death was past, life not come; so he waited. Awhile
    his right hand

Held the brow, helped the eyes left too vacant forth-
    with to remand

To their place what new objects should enter: 't was
    Saul as before.

I looked up and dared gaze at those eyes, nor was
    hurt any more

Than by slow pallid sunsets in autumn, ye watch from
    the shore,

At their sad level gaze o'er the ocean—a sun's slow
    decline

Over hills which, resolved in stern silence, o'erlap and
    entwine

Base with base to knit strength more intensely; so,
    arm folded arm

O'er the chest whose slow heavings subsided.

What spell or what charm,
(For awhile there was trouble within me,) what next
    should I urge
To sustain him where song had restored him?—Song
    filled to the verge
His cup with the wine of this life, pressing all that it
    yields
Of mere fruitage, the strength and the beauty: be-
    yond, on what fields,
Glean a vintage more potent and perfect to brighten
    the eye
And bring blood to the lip, and commend them the
    cup they put by?
He saith, "It is good;" still he drinks not: he lets me
    praise life,
Gives assent, yet would die for his own part.

Then fancies grew rife
Which had come long ago on the pasture, when round
    me the sheep
Fed in silence—above, the one eagle wheeled slow as
    in sleep;
And I lay in my hollow and mused on the world that
    might lie
'Neath his ken, though I saw but the strip 'twixt the
    hill and the sky:

And I laughed—"Since my days are ordained to be
     passed with my flocks,

Let me people at least, with my fancies, the plains and
     the rocks,

Dream the life I am never to mix with, and image
     the show

Of mankind as they live in those fashions I hardly
     shall know!

Schemes of life, its best rules and right uses, the cour-
     age that gains,

And the prudence that keeps what men strive for."
     And now these old trains

Of vague thought came again; I grew surer; so, once
     more the string

Of my harp made response to my spirit, as thus—

       "Yea, my King,"

I began—"thou dost well in rejecting mere comforts
     that spring

From the mere mortal life held in common by man
     and by brute:

In our flesh grows the branch of this life, in our soul
     it bears fruit.

Thou hast marked the slow rise of the tree,—how its
     stem trembled first

Till it passed the kid's lip, the stag's antler; then
     safely outburst

The fan-branches all round; and thou mindest when
these too, in turn,

Broke a-bloom and the palm-tree seemed perfect: yet
more was to learn,

E'en the good that comes in with the palm-fruit. Our
dates shall we slight,

When their juice brings a cure for all sorrow? or care
for the plight

Of the palm's self whose slow growth produced them?
Not so! stem and branch

Shall decay, nor be known in their place, while the
palm-wine shall stanch

Every wound of man's spirit in winter. I pour thee
such wine.

Leave the flesh to the fate it was fit for! the spirit be
thine!

By the spirit, when age shall o'ercome thee, thou still
shalt enjoy

More indeed, than at first when inconscious, the life
of a boy.

Crush that life, and behold its wine running! Each
deed thou hast done

Dies, revives, goes to work in the world; until e'en as
the sun

Looking down on the earth, though clouds spoil him,
though tempests efface,

Can find nothing his own deed produced not, must
  everywhere trace

The results of his past summer-prime,—so, each ray
  of thy will,

Every flash of thy passion and prowess, long over,
  shall thrill

Thy whole people, the countless, with ardor, till they
  too give forth

A like cheer to their sons, who in turn, fill the South
  and the North

With the radiance thy deed was the germ of. Carouse
  in the past!

But the license of age has its limit; thou diest at last:

As the lion when age dims his eyeball, the rose at her
  height,

So with man—so his power and his beauty forever
  take flight.

No! Again a long draught of my soul-wine! Look
  forth o'er the years!

Thou hast done now with eyes for the actual; begin
  with the seer's!

Is Saul dead? In the depth of the vale make his
  tomb—bid arise

A gray mountain of marble heaped four-square, till,
  built to the skies,

Let it mark where the great First King slumbers;
  whose fame would ye know?

Up above see the rock's naked face, where the record
    shall go

In great characters cut by the scribe,—Such was Saul,
    so he did;

With the sages directing the work, by the populace
    chid,—

For not half, they'll affirm, is comprised there! Which
    fault to amend,

In the grove with his kind grows the cedar, whereon
    they shall spend

(See, in tablets 't is level before them) their praise,
    and record

With the gold of the graver, Saul's story,—the states-
    man's great word

Side by side with the poet's sweet comment. The
    river's a-wave

With smooth paper-reeds grazing each other when
    prophet-winds rave:

So the pen gives unborn generations their due and
    their part

In thy being! Then, first of the mighty, thank God
    that thou art!"

And behold while I sang . . . but O Thou who didst
    grant me that day,

And before it not seldom hast granted thy help to
    essay;

Carry on and complete an adventure,—my shield and
    my sword

In that act where my soul was thy servant, thy word
    was my word,—

Still be with me, who then at the summit of human
    endeavor

And scaling the highest, man's thought could, gazed
    hopeless as ever

On the new stretch of heaven above me—till, mighty
    to save,

Just one lift of thy hand cleared that distance—God's
    throne from man's grave!

Let me tell out my tale to its ending—my voice to
    my heart

Which can scarce dare believe in what marvels last
    night I took part,

As this morning I gather the fragments, alone with
    my sheep,

And still fear lest the terrible glory evanish like
    sleep!

For I wake in the gray dewy covert, while Hebron
    upheaves

The dawn struggling with night on his shoulder, and
    Kidron retrieves

Slow the damage of yesterday's sunshine.

                                      I say then,—my song
While I sang thus, assuring the monarch, and ever
        more strong
Made a proffer of good to console him—he slowly
        resumed
His old motions and habitudes kingly. The right
        hand replumed
His black locks to their wonted composure, adjusted
        the swathes
Of his turban, and see—the huge sweat that his coun-
        tenance bathes,
He wipes off with the robe; and he girds now his loins
        as of yore,
And feels slow for the armlets of price, with the clasp
        set before.
He is Saul, ye remember in glory,—ere error had bent
The broad brow from the daily communion; and still,
        though much spent
Be the life and the bearing that front you, the same,
        God did choose,
To receive what a man may waste, desecrate, never
        quite lose.
So sank he along by the tent-prop till, stayed by the
        pile
Of his armor and war-cloak and garments, he leaned
        there awhile.

And sat out my singing,—one arm round the tent-
    prop, to raise

His bent head, and the other hung slack—till I
    touched on the praise

I foresaw from all men in all time, to the man patient
    there;

And thus ended, the harp falling forward. Then first
    I was 'ware

That he sat, as I say, with my head just above his
    vast knees

Which were thrust out on each side around me, like
    oak roots which please

To encircle a lamb when it slumbers. I looked up
    to know

If the best I could do had brought solace: he spoke
    not, but slow

Lifted up the hand slack at his side, till he laid it
    with care

Soft and grave, but in mild settled will, on my brow:
    through my hair

The large fingers were pushed, and he bent back my
    head, with kind power—

All my face back, intent to peruse it, as men do a
    flower.

Thus held he me there with his great eyes that scruti
    nized mine—

And oh, all my heart how it loved him! but where
    was the sign?

I yearned—"Could I help thee, my father, inventing
    a bliss,

I would add, to that life of the past, both the future
    and this;

I would give thee new life altogether, as good, ages
    hence,

As this moment,—had love but the warrant, love's
    heart to dispense!"

Then the truth came upon me. No harp more—no
    song more! outbroke—

"I have gone the whole round of creation: I saw and
    I spoke:

I, a work of God's hand for that purpose, received in
    my brain

And pronounced on the rest of his handwork—re-
    turned him again

His creation's approval or censure: I spoke as I saw:

I report, as a man may of God's work—all's love, yet
    all's law.

Now I lay down the judgeship he lent me. Each
    faculty tasked

To perceive him, has gained an abyss, where a dew-
    drop was asked.

Have I knowledge? confounded it shrivels at Wisdom
  laid bare.

Have I forethought? how purblind, how blank, to the
  Infinite Care!

Do I task any faculty highest, to image success?

I but open my eyes,—and perfection, no more and no
  less,

In the kind I imagined, full-fronts me, and God is
  seen God

In the star, in the stone, in the flesh, in the soul and
  the clod.

And thus looking within and around me, I ever renew

(With that stoop of the soul which in bending up-
  raises it too)

The submission of man's nothing-perfect to God's all-
  complete,

As by each new obeisance in spirit, I climb to his feet.

Yet with all this abounding experience, this deity
  known,

I shall dare to discover some province, some gift of
  my own.

There's a faculty pleasant to exercise, hard to hood-
  wink,

I am fain to keep still in abeyance, (I laugh as I
  think)

Lest, insisting to claim and parade in it, wot ye, I
  worst

E'en the Giver in one gift.—Behold, I could love if I
    durst!

But I sink the pretension as fearing a man may o'er-
    take

God's own speed in the one way of love: I abstain
    for love's sake.

—What, my soul? see thus far and no farther? when
    doors great and small,

Nine-and-ninety flew ope at our touch, should the
    hundredth appall?

In the least things have faith, yet distrust in the
    greatest of all?

Do I find love so full in my nature, God's ultimate
    gift,

That I doubt his own love can compete with it? Here,
    the parts shift?

Here, the creature surpass the Creator,—the end, what
    Began?

Would I fain in my impotent yearning do all for this
    man,

And dare doubt he alone shall not help him, who yet
    alone can?

Would it ever have entered my mind, the bare will,
    much less power.

To bestow on this Saul what I sang of, the marvel-
    lous dower

Of the life he was gifted and filled with? to make
    such a soul,

Such a body, and then such an earth for insphering
    the whole?

And doth it not enter my mind (as my warm tears
    attest)

These good things being given, to go on, and give one
    more, the best?

Ay, to save and redeem and restore him, maintain at
    the height

This perfection,—succeed with life's day-spring,
    death's minute of night?

Interpose at the difficult minute, snatch Saul the
    mistake,

Saul the failure, the ruin he seems now,—and bid him
    awake

From the dream, the probation, the prelude, to find
    himself set

Clear and safe in new light and new life,—a new
    harmony yet

To be run, and continued, and ended—who knows?—
    or endure!

The man taught enough by life's dream, of the rest
    to make sure;

By the pain-throb, triumphantly winning intensified
    bliss,

And the next world's reward and repose, by the strug-
    gles in this.

"I believe it! 'T is thou, God, that givest, 't is I who
  receive:

In the first is the last, in thy will is my power to
  believe.

All's one gift: thou canst grant it moreover, as prompt
  to my prayer

As I breathe out this breath, as I open these arms to
  the air.

From thy will stream the worlds, life and nature, thy
  dread Sabaoth:

I will?—the mere atoms despise me! Why am I not
  loth

To look that, even that in the face too? Why is it
  I dare

Think but lightly of such impuissance? What stops
  my despair?

This;—'t is not what man Does which exalts him, but
  what man Would do!

See the King—I would help him but cannot, the wishes
  fall through.

Could I wrestle to raise him from sorrow, grow poor
  to enrich,

To fill up his life, starve my own out, I would—knowing which,

I know that my service is perfect. Oh, speak through
  me now!

Would I suffer for him that I love? So wouldst thou
    —so wilt thou!

So shall crown thee the topmost, ineffablest, uttermost
    crown—

And thy love fill infinitude wholly, nor leave up nor
    down

One spot for the creature to stand in! It is by no
    breath,

Turn of eye, wave of hand, that salvation joins issue
    with death!

As thy Love is discovered almighty, almighty be
    proved

Thy power, that exists with and for it, of being Be-
    loved!

He who did most, shall bear most; the strongest shall
    stand the most weak.

'T is the weakness in strength, that I cry for! my
    flesh, that I seek

In the Godhead! I seek and I find it. O Saul, it
    shall be

A Face like my face that receives thee; a Man like
    to me,

Thou shalt love and be loved by, forever: a Hand
    like this hand

Shall throw open the gates of new life to thee! See
    the Christ stand!"

I know not too well how I found my way home in
  the night.

There were witnesses, cohorts about me, to left and
  to right,

Angels, powers, the unuttered, unseen, the alive, the
  aware:

I repressed, I got through them as hardly, as strug-
  glingly there,

As a runner beset by the populace famished for
  news—

Life or death. The whole earth was awakened, hell
  loosed with her crews;

And the stars of night beat with emotion, and tingled
  and shot

Out in fire the strong pain of pent knowledge: but I
  fainted not,

For the Hand still impelled me at once and supported,
  suppressed

All the tumult, and quenched it with quiet, and holy
  behest,

Till the rapture was shut in itself, and the earth sank
  to rest.

Anon at the dawn, all that trouble had withered from
  earth—

Not so much, but I saw it die out in the day's tender
  birth;

In the gathered intensity brought to the gray of the
  hills;

In the shuddering forests' held breath; in the sudden
    wind-thrills;

In the startled wild beasts that bore off, each with eye
    sidling still

Though averted with wonder and dread; in the birds
    stiff and chill

That rose heavily, as I approached them, made stupid
    with awe:

E'en the serpent that slid away silent,—he felt the
    new law.

The same stared in the white humid faces upturned
    by the flowers;

The same worked in the heart of the cedar and moved
    the vine-bowers:

And the little brooks witnessing murmured, persistent
    and low,

With their obstinate, all but hushed voices—"E'en so,
    it is so!"

AN EPISTLE

CONTAINING THE STRANGE MEDICAL EXPERIENCE OF
KARSHISH, THE ARAB PHYSICIAN

KARSHISH, the picker-up of learning's crumbs,
The not-incurious in God's handiwork
(This man's-flesh he hath admirably made,

Blown like a bubble, kneaded like a paste,
To coop up and keep down on earth a space
That puff of vapor from his mouth, man's soul)
—To Abib, all-sagacious in our art,
Breeder in me of what poor skill I boast,
Like me inquisitive how pricks and cracks
Befall the flesh through too much stress and strain,
Whereby the wily vapor fain would slip
Back and rejoin its source before the term,—
And aptest in contrivance (under God)
To baffle it by deftly stopping such:—
The vagrant Scholar to his Sage at home
Sends greeting (health and knowledge, fame with
　　　　peace)
Three samples of true snake-stone—rarer still,
One of the other sort, the melon-shaped,
(But fitter, pounded fine, for charms than drugs)
And writeth now the twenty-second time.

　My journeyings were brought to Jericho:
Thus I resume. Who studious in our art
Shall count a little labor unrepaid?
I have shed sweat enough, left flesh and bone
On many a flinty furlong of this land.
Also, the country-side is all on fire
With rumors of a marching hitherward:

Some say Vespasian cometh, some, his son.
A black lynx snarled and pricked a tufted ear;
Lust of my blood inflamed his yellow balls:
I cried and threw my staff and he was gone.
'Twice have the robbers stripped and beaten me,
And once a town declared me for a spy;
But at the end, I reach Jerusalem,
Since this poor covert where I pass the night,
This Bethany, lies scarce the distance thence
A man with plague-sores at the third degree
Runs till he drops down dead. Thou laughest here!
'Sooth, it elates me, thus reposed and safe,
To void the stuffing of my travel-scrip
And share with thee whatever Jewry yields.
A viscid choler is observable
In tertians, I was nearly bold to say;
And falling-sickness hath a happier cure
Than our school wots of: there 's a spider here
Weaves no web, watches on the ledge of tombs,
Sprinkled with mottles on an ash-gray back;
Take five and drop them . . . but who knows his
      mind,
The Syrian runagate I trust this to?
His service payeth me a sublimate
Blown up his nose to help the ailing eye.
Best wait: I reach Jerusalem at morn,

There set in order my experiences,
Gather what most deserves, and give thee all—
Or I might add, Judæa's gum-tragacanth
Scales off in purer flakes, shines clearer-grained,
Cracks 'twixt the pestle and the porphyry,
In fine exceeds our produce. Scalp-disease
Confounds me, crossing so with leprosy—
Thou hadst admired one sort I gained at Zoar—
But zeal outruns discretion. Here I end.

Yet stay: my Syrian blinketh gratefully,
Protesteth his devotion is my price—
Suppose I write what harms not, though he steal?
I half resolve to tell thee, yet I blush,
What set me off a-writing first of all.
An itch I had, a sting to write, a tang!
For, be it this town's barrenness—or else
The Man had something in the look of him—
His case has struck me far more than 't is worth.
So, pardon if—(lest presently I lose
In the great press of novelty at hand
The care and pains this somehow stole from me)
I bid thee take the thing while fresh in mind,
Almost in sight—for, wilt thou have the truth?
The very man is gone from me but now,
Whose ailment is the subject of discourse.
Thus then, and let thy better wit help all!

'T is but a case of mania—subinduced
By epilepsy, at the turning-point
Of trance prolonged unduly some three days:
When, by the exhibition of some drug
Or spell, exorcization, stroke of art
Unknown to me and which 't were well to know,
The evil thing out-breaking all at once
Left the man whole and sound of body indeed,—
But, flinging (so to speak) life's gates too wide,
Making a clear house of it too suddenly,
The first conceit that entered might inscribe
Whatever it was minded on the wall
So plainly at that vantage, as it were,
(First come, first served) that nothing subsequent
Attaineth to erase those fancy-scrawls
The just-returned and new-established soul
Hath gotten now so thoroughly by heart
That henceforth she will read or these or none.
And first—the man's own firm conviction rests
That he was dead (in fact they buried him)
—That he was dead and then restored to life
By a Nazarene physician of his tribe:
—'Sayeth, the same bade "Rise," and he did rise.
"Such cases are diurnal," thou wilt cry.
Not so this figment!—not, that such a fume,
Instead of giving way to time and health,

Should eat itself into the life of life,
As saffron tingeth flesh, blood, bones and all!
For see, how he takes up the after-life.
The man—it is one Lazarus a Jew,
Sanguine, proportioned, fifty years of age,
The body's habit wholly laudable,
As much, indeed, beyond the common health
As he were made and put aside to show.
Think, could we penetrate by any drug
And bathe the wearied soul and worried flesh,
And bring it clear and fair, by three days' sleep!
Whence has the man the balm that brightens all?
This grown man eyes the world now like a child.
Some elders of his tribe, I should premise,
Led in their friend, obedient as a sheep,
To bear my inquisition. While they spoke,
Now sharply, now with sorrow,—told the case,—
He listened not except I spoke to him,
But folded his two hands and let them talk,
Watching the flies that buzzed: and yet no fool.
And that 's a sample how his years must go.
Look, if a beggar, in fixed middle-life,
Should find a treasure,—can he use the same
With straitened habits and with tastes starved small,
And take at once to his impoverished brain
The sudden element that changes things,

That sets the undreamed-of rapture at his hand
And puts the cheap old joy in the scorned dust?
Is he not such an one as moves to mirth—
Warily parsimonious, when no need,
Wasteful as drunkenness at undue times?
All prudent counsel as to what befits
The golden mean, is lost on such an one:
The man's fantastic will is the man's law.
So here—we call the treasure knowledge, say,
Increased beyond the fleshly faculty—
Heaven opened to a soul while yet on earth,
Earth forced on a soul's use while seeing heaven:
The man is witless of the size, the sum,
The value in proportion of all things,
Or whether it be little or be much.
Discourse to him of prodigious armaments
Assembled to besiege his city now,
And of the passing of a mule with gourds—
'T is one! Then take it on the other side,
Speak of some trifling fact,—he will gaze rapt
With stupor at its very littleness,
(Far as I see) as if in that indeed
He caught prodigious import, whole results;
And so will turn to us the bystanders
In ever the same stupor (note this point)
That we too see not with his opened eyes.

Wonder and doubt come wrongly into play,
Preposterously, at cross purposes.
Should his child sicken unto death,—why, look
For scarce abatement of his cheerfulness,
Or pretermission of the daily craft!
While a word, gesture, glance from that same child
At play or in the school or laid asleep
Will startle him to an agony of fear,
Exasperation, just as like. Demand
The reason why—" 't is but a word," object—
"A gesture"—he regards thee as our lord
Who lived there in the pyramid alone,
Looked at us (dost thou mind?) when, being young,
We both would unadvisedly recite
Some charm's beginning, from that book of his,
Able to bid the sun throb wide and burst
All into stars, as suns grown old are wont.
Thou and the child have each a veil alike
Thrown o'er your heads, from under which ye both
Stretch your blind hands and trifle with a match
Over a mine of Greek fire, did ye know!
He holds on firmly to some thread of life—
(It is the life to lead perforcedly)
Which runs across some vast distracting orb
Of glory on either side that meagre thread,
Which, conscious of, he must not enter yet—

The spiritual life around the earthly life:
The law of that is known to him as this,
His heart and brain move there, his feet stay here.
So is the man perplext with impulses
Sudden to start off crosswise, not straight on,
Proclaiming what is right and wrong across,
And not along, this black thread through the blaze—
"It should be" balked by "here it cannot be."
And oft the man's soul springs into his face
As if he saw again and heard again
His sage that bade him "Rise" and he did rise.
Something, a word, a tick o' the blood within
Admonishes: then back he sinks at once
To ashes, who was very fire before,
In sedulous recurrence to his trade
Whereby he earneth him the daily bread;
And studiously the humbler for that pride,
Professedly the faultier that he knows
God's secret, while he holds the thread of life.
Indeed the especial marking of the man
Is prone submission to the heavenly will—
Seeing it, what it is, and why it is.
'Sayeth, he will wait patient to the last
For that same death which must restore his being
To equilibrium, body loosening soul
Divorced even now by premature full growth:

He will live, nay, it pleaseth him to live
So long as God please, and just how God please.
He even seeketh not to please God more
(Which meaneth, otherwise) than as God please.
Hence, I perceive not he affects to preach
The doctrine of his sect whate'er it be,
Make proselytes as madmen thirst to do:
How can he give his neighbor the real ground,
His own conviction? Ardent as he is—
Call his great truth a lie, why, still the old
"Be it as God please" reassureth him.
I probed the sore as thy disciple should:
"How, beast," said I, "this stolid carelessness
Sufficeth thee, when Rome is on her march
To stamp out like a little spark thy town,
Thy tribe, thy crazy tale and thee at once?"
He merely looked with his large eyes on me.
The man is apathetic, you deduce?
Contrariwise, he loves both old and young,
Able and weak, affects the very brutes
And birds—how say I? flowers of the field—
As a wise workman recognizes tools
In a master's workshop, loving what they make.
Thus is the man as harmless as a lamb:
Only impatient, let him do his best,
At ignorance and carelessness and sin—

An indignation which is promptly curbed:
As when in certain travel I have feigned
To be an ignoramus in our art
According to some preconceived design,
And happed to hear the land's practitioners,
Steeped in conceit sublimed by ignorance,
Prattle fantastically on disease,
Its cause and cure—and I must hold my peace!

   Thou wilt object—why have I not ere this
Sought out the sage himself, the Nazarene
Who wrought this cure, inquiring at the source,
Conferring with the frankness that befits?
Alas! it grieveth me, the learned leech
Perished in a tumult many years ago,
Accused—our learning's fate—of wizardry,
Rebellion, to the setting up a rule
And creed prodigious as described to me.
His death, which happened when the earthquake fell
(Prefiguring, as soon appeared, the loss
To occult learning in our lord the sage
Who lived there in the pyramid alone)
Was wrought by the mad people—that 's their wont!
On vain recourse, as I conjecture it,
To his tried virtue, for miraculous help—
How could he stop the earthquake? That's their way!

The other imputations must be lies:
But take one, though I loathe to give it thee,
In mere respect for any good man's fame.
(And after all, our patient Lazarus
Is stark mad; should we count on what he says?
Perhaps not: though in writing to a leech
'T is well to keep back nothing of a case.)
This man so cured regards the curer, then,
As—God forgive me! who but God himself,
Creator and sustainer of the world,
That came and dwelt in flesh on it awhile!
—'Sayeth that such an one was born and lived,
Taught, healed the sick, broke bread at his own house,
Then died, with Lazarus by, for aught I know,
And yet was . . . what I said nor choose repeat.
And must have so avouched himself, in fact,
In hearing of this very Lazarus
Who saith—but why all this of what he saith?
Why write of trivial matters, things of price
Calling at every moment for remark?
I noticed on the margin of a pool
Blue-flowering borage, the Aleppo sort,
Aboundeth, very nitrous. It is strange!

　Thy pardon for this long and tedious case,
Which, now that I review it, needs must seem

Unduly dwelt on, prolixly set forth!
Nor I myself discern in what is writ
Good cause for the peculiar interest
And awe indeed this man has touched me with
Perhaps the journey's end, the weariness
Had wrought upon me first. I met him thus:
I crossed a ridge of short sharp broken hills
Like an old lion's cheek teeth. Out there came
A moon made like a face with certain spots
Multiform, manifold, and menacing:
Then a wind rose behind me. So we met
In this old sleepy town at unaware,
The man and I. I send thee what is writ.
Regard it as a chance, a matter risked
To this ambiguous Syrian—he may lose,
Or steal, or give it thee with equal good.
Jerusalem's repose shall make amends
For time this letter wastes, thy time and mine;
Till when, once more thy pardon and farewell!

The very God! think, Abib; dost thou think?
So, the All-Great, were the All-Loving too—
So, through the thunder comes a human voice
Saying, "O heart I made, a heart beats here!
Face, my hands fashioned, see it in myself!
Thou hast no power nor mayst conceive of mine,

But love I gave thee, with myself to love,
And thou must love me who have died for thee!"
The madman saith He said so: it is strange.

***

FRA LIPPO LIPPI

I AM poor brother Lippo, by your leave!
You need not clap your torches to my face.
Zooks, what 's to blame? you think you see a monk
What, 't is past midnight, and you go the rounds,
And here you catch me at an alley's end
Where sportive ladies leave their doors ajar?
The Carmine 's my cloister: hunt it up.
Do,—harry out, if you must show your zeal,
Whatever rat, there, haps on his wrong hole,
And nip each softling of a wee white mouse,
Weke, weke, that 's crept to keep him company!
Aha, you know your betters! Then, you 'll take
Your hand away that 's fiddling on my throat,
And please to know me likewise. Who am I?
Why, one, sir, who is lodging with a friend
Three streets off—he's a certain . . . how d' ye call?
Master—a . . . Cosimo of the Medici,
I' the house that caps the corner. Boh! you were best!
Remember and tell me, the day you 're hanged,

How you affected such a gullet's-gripe!
But you, sir, it concerns you that your knaves
Pick up a manner nor discredit you:
Zooks, are we pilchards, that they sweep the streets
And count fair prize what comes into their net?
He 's Judas to a tittle, that man is!
Just such a face! Why, sir, you make amends.
Lord, I 'm not angry! Bid your hangdogs go
Drink out this quarter-florin to the health
Of the munificent House that harbors me
(And many more beside, lads! more beside!)
And all 's come square again. I 'd like his face—
His, elbowing on his comrade in the door
With the pike and lantern,—for the slave that holds
John Baptist's head a-dangle by the hair
With one hand ("Look you, now," as who should say)
And his weapon in the other, yet unwiped!
It 's not your chance to have a bit of chalk,
A wood-coal or the like? or you should see!
Yes, I'm the painter, since you style me so.
What, brother Lippo's doings, up and down,
You know them and they take you? like enough!
I saw the proper twinkle in your eye—
'Tell you, I liked your looks at very first.
Let 's sit and set things straight now, hip to haunch.
Here 's spring come, and the nights one makes up
        bands

To roam the town and sing out carnival,
And I 've been three weeks shut within my mew.
A-painting for the great man, saints and saints
And saints again. I could not paint all night—
Ouf! I leaned out of window for fresh air.
There came a hurry of feet and little feet,
A sweep of lute-strings, laughs, and whiffs of song,—
Flower o' the broom,
Take away love, and our earth is a tomb!
Flower o' the quince,
I let Lisa go, and what good in life since?
Flower o' the thyme—and so on. Round they went.
Scarce had they turned the corner when a titter
Like the skipping of rabbits by moonlight,—three slim
        shapes,
And a face that looked up . . . zooks, sir, flesh and
        blood,
That 's all I 'm made of! Into shreds it went,
Curtain and counterpane and coverlet,
All the bed-furniture—a dozen knots,
There was a ladder! Down I let myself,
Hands and feet, scrambling somehow, and so dropped,
And after them. I came up with the fun
Hard by Saint Laurence, hail fellow, well met,—
Flower o' the rose,
If I 've been merry, what matter who knows?

And so as I was stealing back again
To get to bed and have a bit of sleep
Ere I rise up to-morrow and go work
On Jerome knocking at his poor old breast
With his great round stone to subdue the flesh,
You snap me of the sudden. Ah, I see!
Though your eye twinkles still, you shake your head—
Mine 's shaved—a monk, you say—the sting 's in that!
If Master Cosimo announced himself,
Mum 's the word naturally; but a monk!
Come, what am I a beast for? tell us, now!
I was a baby when my mother died
And father died and left me in the street.
I starved there, God knows how, a year or two
On fig-skins, melon-parings, rinds and shucks,
Refuse and rubbish. One fine frosty day,
My stomach being empty as your hat,
The wind doubled me up and down I went.
Old Aunt Lapaccia trussed me with one hand,
(Its fellow was a stinger as I knew)
And so along the wall, over the bridge,
By the straight cut to the convent. Six words there,
While I stood munching my first bread that month:
"So, boy, you 're minded," quoth the good fat father,
Wiping his own mouth, 't was refection-time,—
"To quit this very miserable world?

Will you renounce" . . . "the mouthful of bread?"
      thought I;
By no means! Brief, they made a monk of me;
I did renounce the world, its pride and greed,
Palace, farm, villa, shop, and banking-house,
Trash, such as these poor devils of Medici
Have given their hearts to—all at eight years old.
Well, sir, I found in time, you may be sure,
'T was not for nothing—the good bellyful,
The warm serge and the rope that goes all round,
And day-long blessed idleness beside!
"Let 's see what the urchin 's fit for"—that came next.
Not overmuch their way, I must confess.
Such a to-do! They tried me with their books;
Lord, they 'd have taught me Latin in pure waste!
Flower o' the clove,
All the Latin I construe is "amo," I love!
But, mind you, when a boy starves in the streets
Eight years together, as my fortune was,
Watching folk's faces to know who will fling
The bit of half-stripped grape-bunch he desires,
And who will curse or kick him for his pains,—
Which gentleman processional and fine,
Holding a candle to the Sacrament,
Will wink and let him lift a plate and catch

The droppings of the wax to sell again,
Or holla for the Eight and have him whipped,—
How say I?—nay, which dog bites, which lets **drop**
His bone from the heap of offal in the street,—
Why, soul and sense of him grew sharp alike,
He learns the look of things, and none the less
For admonition from the hunger-pinch.
I had a store of such remarks, be sure,
Which, after I found leisure, turned to use.
I drew men's faces on my copy-books,
Scrawled them within the antiphonary's **marge,**
Joined legs and arms to the long music-notes,
Found eyes and nose and chin for A's and B's,
And made a string of pictures of the world
Betwixt the ins and outs of verb and noun,
On the wall, the bench, the door. The monks **looked**
     black.
"Nay," quoth the Prior, "turn him out, d' ye **say?**
In no wise. Lose a crow and catch a lark.
What if at last we get our man of parts,
We Carmelites, like those Camaldolese
And Preaching Friars, to do our church up **fine**
And put the front on it that ought to be!"
And hereupon he bade me daub away.
Thank you! my head being crammed, the walls
     blank,

Never was such prompt disemburdening.
First, every sort of monk, the black and white,
I drew them, fat and lean: then, folk at church,
From good old gossips waiting to confess
Their cribs of barrel-droppings, candle-ends,—
To the breathless fellow at the altar-foot,
Fresh from his murder, safe and sitting there

  With the little children round him in a row
Of admiration, half for his beard and half
For that white anger of his victim's son
Shaking a fist at him with one fierce arm,
Signing himself with the other because of Christ
(Whose sad face on the cross sees only this
After the passion of a thousand years)
Till some poor girl, her apron o'er her head,
(Which the intense eyes looked through) came at eve
On tiptoe, said a word, dropped in a loaf,
Her pair of earrings and a bunch of flowers
(The brute took growling), prayed, and so was gone.
I painted all, then cried " 'T is ask and have;
Choose, for more 's ready!"—laid the ladder flat,
And showed my covered bit of cloister-wall.
The monks closed in a circle and praised loud
Till checked, taught what to see and not to see,
Being simple bodies,—"That 's the very man!

Look at the boy who stoops to pat the dog!
That woman 's like the Prior's niece who comes
To care about his asthma: it 's the life!"
But there my triumph's straw-fire flared and funked;
Their betters took their turn to see and say:
The Prior and the learned pulled a face
And stopped all that in no time. "How? what 's here?
Quite from the mark of painting, bless us all!
Faces, arms, legs, and bodies like the true
As much as pea and pea! it 's devil's-game!
Your business is not to catch men with show,
With homage to the perishable clay,
But lift them over it, ignore it all,
Make them forget there 's such a thing as flesh.
Your business is to paint the souls of men—
Man's soul, and it 's a fire, smoke . . . no, it 's not . . .
It 's vapor done up like a new-born babe—
(In that shape when you die it leaves your mouth)
It 's . . . well, what matters talking, it 's the soul!
Give us no more of body than shows soul!
Here 's Giotto, with his Saint a-praising God,
That sets us praising,—why not stop with him?
Why put all thoughts of praise out of our head
With wonder at lines, colors, and what not?
Paint the soul, never mind the legs and arms!

Rub all out, try at it a second time.
Oh, that white smallish female with the breasts.
She's just my niece . . . Herodias, I would say,—
Who went and danced and got men's heads cut off!
Have it all out!" Now, is this sense, I ask?
A fine way to paint soul, by painting body
So ill, the eye can't stop there, must go further
And can't fare worse! Thus, yellow does for white
When what you put for yellow 's simply black,
And any sort of meaning looks intense
When all beside itself means and looks naught.
Why can't a painter lift each foot in turn,
Left foot and right foot, go a double step,
Make his flesh liker and his soul more like,
Both in their order? Take the prettiest face,
The Prior's niece . . . patron-saint—is it so pretty
You can't discover if it means hope, fear,
Sorrow or joy? won't beauty go with these?
Suppose I 've made her eyes all right and blue,
Can't I take breath and try to add life's flash,
And then add soul and heighten them three-fold?
Or say there 's beauty with no soul at all—
(I never saw it—put the case the same—)
If you get simple beauty and naught else,
You get about the best thing God invents:

That 's somewhat: and you 'll find the soul you have
    missed,
Within yourself, when you return him thanks.
"Rub all out!" Well, well, there 's my life, in short,
And so the thing has gone on ever since.
I 'm grown a man no doubt, I 've broken bounds:
You should not take a fellow eight years old
And make him swear to never kiss the girls.
I'm my own master, paint now as I please—
Having a friend, you see, in the Corner-house!
Lord, it 's fast holding by the rings in front—
Those great rings serve more purposes than just
To plant a flag in, or tie up a horse!
And yet the old schooling sticks, the old grave eyes
Are peeping o'er my shoulder as I work,
The heads shake still—"It 's art's decline, my son!
You 're not of the true painters, great and old;
Brother Angelico 's the man, you 'll find;
Brother Lorenzo stands his single peer:
Fag on at flesh, you 'll never make the third!"
Flower o' the pine,
You keep your mistr . . . manners, and I'll stick to
    mine!
I'm not the third, then: bless us, they must know!
Don't you think they 're the likeliest to know,

They with their Latin? So, I swallow my rage,
Clench my teeth, suck my lips in tight, and paint
To please them—sometimes do and sometimes don't;
For, doing most, there 's pretty sure to come
A turn, some warm eye finds me at my saints—
A laugh, a cry, the business of the world—
(*Flower o' the peach,*
Death for us all, and his own life for each!)
And my whole soul revolves, the cup runs over,
The world and life 's too big to pass for a dream,
And I do these wild things in sheer despite,
And play the fooleries you catch me at,
In pure rage! The old mill-horse, out at grass
After hard years, throws up his stiff heels so,
Although the miller does not preach to him
The only good of grass is to make chaff.
What would men have? Do they like grass or no—
May they or may n't they? all I want 's the thing
Settled forever one way. As it is,
You tell too many lies and hurt yourself:
You don't like what you only like too much,
You do like what, if given you at your word,
You find abundantly detestable.
For me, I think I speak as I was taught;
I always see the garden and God there

ʌ-making man's wife: and, my lesson learned,
The value and significance of flesh,
I can't unlearn ten minutes afterwards.

You understand me: I 'm a beast, I know.
But see, now—why, I see as certainly
As that the morning-star 's about to shine,
What will hap some day. We 've a youngster here
Comes to our convent, studies what I do,
Slouches and stares and lets no atom drop:
His name is Guidi—he 'll not mind the monks—
They call him Hulking Tom, he lets them talk—
He picks my practice up—he 'll paint apace,
I hope so—though I never live so long,
I know what 's sure to follow. You be judge!
You speak no Latin more than I, belike;
However, you 're my man, you 've seen the world
—The beauty and the wonder and the power,
The shapes of things, their colors, lights and shades,
Changes, surprises,—and God made it all!
—For what? Do you feel thankful, ay or no,
For this fair town's face, yonder river's line,
The mountain round it and the sky above,
Much more the figures of man, woman, child,
These are the frame to? What 's it all about?

To be passed over, despised? or dwelt upon,
Wondered at? oh, this last of course!—you say.
But why not do as well as say,—paint these
Just as they are, careless what comes of it?
God's works—paint any one, and count it crime
To let a truth slip. Don't object, "His works
Are here already; nature is complete:
Suppose you reproduce her—(which you can't)
There 's no advantage! you must beat her, then."
For, don't you mark? we 're made so that we love
First when we see them painted, things we have passed
Perhaps a hundred times nor cared to see;
And so they are better, painted—better to us,
Which is the same thing. Art was given for that;
God uses us to help each other so,
Lending our minds out. Have you noticed, now,
Your cullion's hanging face? A bit of chalk,
And trust me but you should, though! How much
          more,
If I drew higher things with the same truth!
That were to take the Prior's pulpit-place,
Interpret God to all of you! Oh, oh,
It makes me mad to see what men shall do
And we in our graves! This world 's no blot for us,
Nor blank; it means intensely, and means good:

To find its meaning is my meat and drink.
"Ay, but you don't so instigate to prayer!"
Strikes in the Prior: "when your meaning 's plain
It does not say to folk—remember matins,
Or, mind you fast next Friday!" Why, for this
What need of art at all? A skull and bones,
Two bits of stick nailed crosswise, or, what's best,
A bell to chime the hour with, does as well.
I painted a Saint Laurence six months since
At Prato, splashed the fresco in fine style:
"How looks my painting, now the scaffold 's down?"
I ask a brother: "Hugely," he returns—
"Already not one phiz of your three slaves
Who turn the Deacon off his toasted side,
But 's scratched and prodded to our heart's content,
The pious people have so eased their own
With coming to say prayers there in a rage:
We get on fast to see the bricks beneath.
Expect another job this time next year,
For pity and religion grow i' the crowd—
Your painting serves its purpose!" Hang the fools!

   —That is—you 'll not mistake an idle word
Spoke in a huff by a poor monk, God wot,
Tasting the air this spicy night which turns

The unaccustomed head like Chianti wine!
Oh, the church knows! don't misreport me, now!
It 's natural a poor monk out of bounds
Should have his apt word to excuse himself:
And hearken how I plot to make amends.
ʹi have bethought me: I shall paint a piece
  . . . There 's for you!   Give me six months, ther
      go, see
Something in Sant' Ambrogio's!   Bless the nuns!
They want a cast o' my office. I shall paint
God in the midst, Madonna and her babe,
Ringed by a bowery, flowery angel-brood,
Lilies and vestments and white faces, sweet
As puff on puff of grated orris-root
When ladies crowd to Church at midsummer.
And then i' the front, of course a saint or two—
Saint John, because he saves the Florentines,
Saint Ambrose, who puts down in black and white
The convent's friends and gives them a long day,
And Job, I must have him there past mistake,
The man of Uz (and Us without the z,
Painters who need his patience).   Well, all these
Secured at their devotion, up shall come
Out of a corner when you least expect.
As one by a dark stair into a great light,

Music and talking, who but Lippo! I!—
Mazed, motionless, and moonstruck—I 'm the man!
Back I shrink—what is this I see and hear?
I, caught up with my monk's-things by mistake,
My old serge gown and rope that goes all round,
I, in this presence, this pure company!
Where 's a hole, where 's a corner for escape?
Then steps a sweet angelic slip of a thing
Forward, puts out a soft palm—"Not so fast!"
—Addresses the celestial presence, "nay—
He made you and devised you, after all,
Though he 's none of you! Could Saint John there
    draw—
His camel-hair make up a painting-brush?
We come to brother Lippo for all that,
Iste perfecit opus!" So, all smile—
I shuffle sideways with my blushing face
Under the cover of a hundred wings
Thrown like a spread of kirtles when you 're **gay**
And play hot cockles, all the doors being shut,
Till, wholly unexpected, in there pops
The hothead husband! Thus I scuttle **off**
To some safe bench behind, not letting **go**
The palm of her, the little lily thing
That spoke the good word for me in the nick,

Like the Prior's niece . . . Saint Lucy, I would say.
And so all 's saved for me, and for the church
A pretty picture gained. Go, six months hence!
Your hand, sir, and good-by: no lights, no lights!
The street 's hushed, and I know my own way back,
Don't fear me! There 's the gray beginning Zooks!

ANDREA DEL SARTO

CALLED "THE FAULTLESS PAINTER"

But do not let us quarrel any more,
No, my Lucrezia; bear with me for once:
Sit down and all shall happen as you wish.
You turn your face, but does it bring your heart?
I 'll work then for your friend's friend, never fear,
Treat his own subject after his own way,
Fix his own time, accept too his own price,
And shut the money into this small hand
When next it takes mine. Will it? tenderly?
Oh, I 'll content him,—but to-morrow, Love!
I often am much wearier than you think,
This evening more than usual, and it seems
As if—forgive now—should you let me sit

Here by the window with your hand in mine
And look a half-hour forth on Fiesole,
Both of one mind, as married people use,
Quietly, quietly the evening through,
I might get up to-morrow to my work
Cheerful and fresh as ever. Let us try.
To-morrow, how you shall be glad for this?
Your soft hand is a woman of itself,
And mine the man's bared breast she curls inside.
Don't count the time lost, neither; you must serve
For each of the five pictures we require:
It saves a model. So! keep looking so—
My serpentining beauty, rounds on rounds!
—How could you ever prick those perfect ears,
Even to put the pearl there! oh, so sweet—
My face, my moon, my everybody's moon,
Which everybody looks on and calls his,
And, I suppose, is looked on by in turn,
While she looks—no one's: very dear, no less.
You smile? why, there 's my picture ready made,
There 's what we painters call our harmony!
A common grayness silvers everything,—
All in a twilight, you and I alike
—You, at the point of your first pride in me
(That's gone you know),—but I, at every point;

My youth, my hope, my art, being all toned down
To yonder sober pleasant Fiesole.
There 's the bell clinking from the chapel-top;
That length of convent-wall across the way
Holds the trees safer, huddled more inside;
The last monk leaves the garden; days decrease,
And autumn grows, autumn in everything.
Eh? the whole seems to fall into a shape
As if I saw alike my work and self
And all that I was born to be and do.
A twilight-piece. Love, we are in God's hand.
How strange now looks the life he makes us lead;
So free we seem, so fettered fast we are!
I feel he laid the fetter: let it lie!
This chamber for example—turn your head—
All that 's behind us! You don't understand
Nor care to understand about my art,
But you can hear at least when people speak:
And that cartoon, the second from the door
—It is the thing, Love! so such thing should be—
Behold Madonna!—I am bold to say.
I can do with my pencil what I know,
What I see, what at bottom of my heart
I wish for, if I ever wish so deep—
Do easily, too—when I say, perfectly,

I do not boast, perhaps: yourself are judge,
Who listened to the Legate's talk last week,
And just as much they used to say in France.
At any rate 't is easy, all of it!
No sketches first, no studies, that 's long past:
I do what many dream of all their lives,
—Dream? strive to do, and agonize to do,
And fail in doing. I could count twenty such
On twice your fingers, and not leave this town,
Who strive—you don't know how the others strive
To paint a little thing like that you smeared
Carelessly passing with your robes afloat,—
Yet do much less, so much less, Someone says,
(I know his name, no matter)—so much less!
Well, less is more, Lucrezia: I am judged.
There burns a truer light of God in them,
In their vexed beating stuffed and stopped-up brain,
Heart, or whate'er else, than goes on to prompt
This low-pulsed forthright craftsman's hand of mine.
Their works drop groundward, but themselves, I
        know,
Reach many a time a heaven that 's shut to me,
Enter and take their place there sure enough,
Though they come back and cannot tell the world.
My works are nearer heaven, but I sit here.

The sudden blood of these men! at a word—
Praise them, it boils, or blame them, it boils too.
I, painting from myself and to myself,
Know what I do, am unmoved by men's blame
Or their praise either. Somebody remarks
Morello's outline there is wrongly traced,
His hue mistaken; what of that? or else,
Rightly traced and well ordered; what of that?
Speak as they please, what does the mountain care?
Ah, but a man's reach should exceed his grasp,
Or what's a heaven for? All is silver-gray
Placid and perfect with my art: the worse!
I know both what I want and what might gain,
And yet how profitless to know, to sigh
"Had I been two, another and myself,
Our head would have o'erlooked the world!"
            No doubt.
Yonder 's a work now, of that famous youth
The Urbinate who died five years ago.
('T is copied, George Vasari sent it me.)
Well, I can fancy how he did it all,
Pouring his soul, with kings and popes to see,
Reaching, that heaven might so replenish him,
Above and through his art—for it gives way:
That arm is wrongly put—and there again—

A fault to pardon in the drawing's lines,
Its body, so to speak: its soul is right,
He means right—that, a child may understand.
Still, what an arm! and I could alter it:
But all the play, the insight and the stretch—
Out of me, out of me! And wherefore out?
Had you enjoined them on me, given me soul,
We might have risen to Rafael, I and you!
Nay, love, you did give all I asked, I think—
More than I merit, yes, by many times.
But had you—oh, with the same perfect brow,
And perfect eyes, and more than perfect mouth,
And the low voice my soul hears, as a bird
The fowler's pipe, and follows to the snare—
Had you, with these the same, but brought a mind!
Some women do so. Had the mouth there urged
"God and the glory! never care for gain.
The present by the future, what is that?
Live for fame, side by side with Agnolo!
Rafael is waiting: up to God, all three!"
I might have done it for you. So it seems:
Perhaps not. All is as God overrules.
Beside, incentives come from the soul's self;
The rest avail not. Why do I need you?
What wife had Rafael, or has Agnolo?

In this world, who can do a thing, will not;
And who would do it, cannot, I perceive:
Yet the will 's somewhat—somewhat, too, the power—
And thus we half-men struggle.   At the end,
God, I conclude, compensates, punishes.
'T is safer for me, if the award be strict,
That I am something underrated here,
Poor this long while, despised, to speak the truth.
I dared not, do you know, leave home all day,
For fear of chancing on the Paris lords.
The best is when they pass and look aside;
But they speak sometimes; I must bear it all.
Well may they speak!   That Francis, that first time,
And that long festal year at Fontainebleau!
I surely then could sometimes leave the ground,
Put on the glory, Rafael's daily wear,
In that humane great monarch's golden look,—
One finger in his beard or twisted curl
Over his mouth's good mark that made the smile,
One arm about my shoulder, round my neck,
The jingle of his gold chain in my ear,
I painting proudly with his breath on me,
All his court round him, seeing with his eyes,
Such frank French eyes, and such a fire of souls
Profuse, my hand kept plying by those hearts.—

And, best of all, this, this, this face beyond,
This in the background, waiting on my work,
To crown the issue with a last reward!
A good time, was it not, my kingly days?
And had you not grown restless . . . but I know—
'T is done and past; 't was right, my instinct said;
Too live the life grew, golden and not gray,
And I 'm the weak-eyed bat no sun should tempt
Out of the grange whose four walls make his world.
How could it end in any other way?
You called me, and I came home to your heart.
The triumph was—to reach and stay there; since
I reached it ere the triumph, what is lost?
Let my hands frame your face in your hair's gold,
You beautiful Lucrezia that are mine!
"Rafael did this, Andrea painted that;
The Roman's is the better when you pray,
But still the other's Virgin was his wife"—
Men will excuse me. I am glad to judge
Both pictures in your presence; clearer grows
My better fortune, I resolve to think.
For, do you know, Lucrezia, as God lives,
Said one day Agnolo, his very self,
To Rafael . . . I have known it all these years . . .
(When the young man was flaming out his thoughts

Upon a palace wall for Rome to see,
Too lifted up in heart because of it)
"Friend, there 's a certain sorry little scrub
Goes up and down our Florence, none cares how,
Who, were he set to plan and execute
As you are, pricked on by your popes and kings,
Would bring the sweat into that brow of yours!"
To Rafael's!—And indeed the arm is wrong.
I hardly dare . . . yet, only you to see,
Give the chalk here—quick, thus the line should go!
Ay, but the soul! he 's Rafael! rub it out!
Still, all I care for, if he spoke the truth,
(What he? why, who but Michel Agnolo?
Do you forget already words like those?)
If really there was such a chance, so lost,—
Is, whether you 're—not grateful—but more pleased.
Well, let me think so. And you smile indeed!
This hour has been an hour! Another smile?
If you would sit thus by me every night
I should work better, do you comprehend?
I mean that I should earn more, give you more.
See, it is settled dusk now; there 's a star;
Morello 's gone, the watch-lights show the wall,
The cue-owls speak the name we call them by.
Come from the window, love,—come in, at last,

Inside the melancholy little house
We built to be so gay with. God is just.
King Francis may forgive me: oft at nights
When I look up from painting, eyes tired out,
The walls become illumined, brick from brick
Distinct, instead of mortar, fierce bright gold
That gold of his I did cement them with!
Let us but love each other. Must you go?
That Cousin here again? he waits outside?
Must see you—you, and not with me? Those loans?
More gaming debts to pay? you smiled for that?
Well, let smiles buy me! have you more to spend?
While hand and eye and something of a heart
Are left me, work 's my ware, and what 's it worth?
I 'll pay my fancy. Only let me sit
The gray remainder of the evening out,
Idle, you call it, and muse perfectly
How I could paint, were I but back in France,
One picture, just one more—the Virgin's face
Not yours this time! I want you at my side
To hear them—that is, Michel Agnolo—
Judge all I do and tell you of its worth.
Will you? To-morrow, satisfy your friend.
I take the subjects for his corridor,
Finish the portrait out of hand—there, there,

And throw him in another thing or two
If he demurs; the whole should prove enough
To pay for this same Cousin's freak. Beside,
What 's better and what 's all I care about,
Get you the thirteen scudi for the ruff!
Love, does that please you? Ah, but what does he,
The Cousin! what does he to please you more?

I am grown peaceful as old age to-night.
I regret little, I would change still less.
Since there my past life lies, why alter it?
The very wrong to Francis!—it is true
I took his coin, was tempted and complied,
And built this house and sinned, and all is said.
My father and my mother died of want.
Well, had I riches of my own? you see
How one gets rich! Let each one bear his lot.
They were born poor, lived poor, and poor they died:
And I have labored somewhat in my time
And not been paid profusely. Some good son
Paint my two hundred pictures—let him try!
No doubt, there 's something strikes a balance.
            Yes,
You loved me quite enough, it seems to-night.
This must suffice me here. What would one have?

In heaven, perhaps, new chances, one more chance—
Four great walls in the New Jerusalem,
Meted on each side by the angel's reed,
For Leonard, Rafael, Agnolo and me
To cover—the three first without a wife,
While I have mine! So—still they overcome
Because there 's still Lucrezia,—as I choose.

Again the Cousin's whistle! Go, my Love.

MASTER HUGUES OF SAXE-GOTHA

Hist, but a word, fair and soft!
    Forth and be judged, Master Hugues!
Answer the question I 've put you so oft:
    What do you mean by your mountainous fugues?
See, we 're alone in the loft,—

I, the poor organist here,
    Hugues, the composer of note,
Dead though, and done with, this many a year;
    Let's have a colloquy, something to quote,
Make the world prick up its ear!

See, the church empties apace:
    Fast they extinguish the lights.

Hallo there, sacristan! Five minutes' grace!
  Here's a crank pedal wants setting to rights,
Balks one of holding the base.

See, our huge house of the sounds,
    Hushing its hundreds at once
Bids the last loiterer back to his bounds!
    —O you may challenge them, not a response
Get the church-saints on their rounds!

(Saints go their rounds, who shall doubt?
    —March, with the moon to admire,
Up nave, down chancel, turn transept about,
    Supervise all betwixt pavement and spire,
Put rats and mice to the rout—

Aloys and Jurien and Just—
    Order things back to their place,
Have a sharp eye lest the candlesticks rust,
    Rub the church-plate, darn the sacrament-lace,
Clear the desk-velvet of dust.)

Here 's your book, younger folks shelve!
    Played I not off-hand and runningly,
Just now, your masterpiece, hard number twelve?
    Here 's what should strike, could one handle it cun-
        ningly:
Help the axe, give it a helve!

Page after page as I played,
  Every bar's rest where one wipes
Sweat from one's brow, I looked up and surveyed,
  O'er my three claviers, yon forest of pipes
Whence you still peeped in the shade.

Sure you were wishful to speak?
  You, with brow ruled like a score,
Yes, and eyes buried in pits on each cheek,
  Like two great breves, as they wrote them of yore,
Each side that bar, your straight beak!

Sure you said—"Good, the mere notes!
  Still, couldst thou take my intent,
Know what procured me our Company's votes—
  A master were lauded and sciolists shent,
Parted the sheep from the goats!"

Well, then, speak up, never flinch!
  Quick, ere my candle 's a snuff
—Burnt, do you see? to its uttermost inch—
  I believe in you, but that 's not enough:
Give my conviction a clinch!

First you deliver your phrase
  —Nothing propound, that I see,
Fit in itself for much blame or much praise—

Answered no less, where no answer needs be;
Off start the Two on their ways.

Straight must a Third interpose,
  Volunteer needlessly help;
In strikes a Fourth, a Fifth thrusts in his nose,
  So the cry 's open, the kennel 's a-yelp,
Argument 's hot to the close.

One dissertates, he is candid;
  Two must discept,—has distinguished;
Three helps the couple, if ever yet man did;
    Four protests; Five makes a dart at the thing
        wished:
Back to One, goes the case bandied.

One says his say with a difference;
  More of expounding, explaining!
All now is wrangle, abuse and vociferance;
  Now there 's a truce, all 's subdued, self-restraining:
Five, though, stands out all the stiffer hence.

One is incisive, corrosive;
  Two retorts, nettled, curt, crepitant;
Three makes rejoinder, expansive, explosives;
  Four overbears them all, strident and strepitant:
Five . . . O Danaides, O Sieve!

Now, they ply axes and crowbars;
  Now, they prick pins at a tissue
Fine as a skein of the casuist Escobar's
  Worked on the bone of a lie. To what issue?
Where is our gain at the Two-bars?

Est fuga, volvitur rota.
  On we drift: where looms the dim port?
One, Two, Three, Four, Five, contribute their quota;
  Something is gained, if one caught but the import—
Show it us, Hugues of Saxe-Gotha!

What with affirming, denying,
  Holding, risposting, subjoining,
All 's like . . . it 's like . . . for an instance I 'm
      trying . . .
  There! See our roof, its gilt moulding and groining
Under those spider-webs lying!

So your fugue broadens and thickens,
  Greatens and deepens and lengthens,
Till we exclaim—"But where 's music, the dickens?
  Blot ye the gold, while your spider-web strengthens
—Blacked to the stoutest of thickens?"

I for man's effort am zealous:
  Prove me such censure unfounded!

Seems it surprising a lover grows jealous—
  Hopes 't was for something, his organ-pipes sounded,
Tiring three boys at the bellows?

Is it your moral of Life?
  Such a web, simple and subtle,
Weave we on earth here in impotent strife,
  Backward and forward each throwing his shuttle,
Death ending all with a knife?

Over our heads truth and nature—
  Still our life's zigzags and dodges,
Ins and outs, weaving a new legislature—
  God's gold just shining its last where that lodges,
Palled beneath man's usurpature.

So we o'ershroud stars and roses,
  Cherub and trophy and garland;
Nothings grow something which quietly closes
  Heaven's earnest eye: not a glimpse of the far land
Gets through our comments and glozes.

Ah, but traditions, inventions,
  (Say we and make up a visage)
So many men with such various intentions,
  Down the past ages, must know more than this age!
Leave we the web its dimensions!

Who thinks Hugues wrote for the deaf,
  Proved a mere mountain in labor?
Better submit; try again; what's the clef?
  'Faith, 't is no trifle for pipe and for tabor—
Four flats, the minor in F.

Friend, your fugue taxes the finger:
  Learning it once, who would lose it?
Yet all the while a misgiving will linger,
  Truth 's golden o'er us although we refuse it—
Nature, through cobwebs we string her.

Hugues! I advise *meâ pœnâ*
  (Counterpoint glares like a Gorgon)
Bid One, Two, Three, Four, Five, clear the arena!
  Say the word, straight I unstop the full organ,
Blare out the *mode Palestrina.*

While in the roof, if I'm right there,
  . . . Lo you, the wick in the socket!
Hallo, you sacristan, show us a light there!
  Down it dips, gone like a rocket.
What, you want, do you, to come unawares,
Sweeping the church up for first morning-prayers,
And find a poor devil has ended his cares
At the foot of your rotten-runged rat-riddled stairs?
  Do I carry the moon in my pocket?

ABT VOGLER

ABT VOGLER

(AFTER HE HAS BEEN EXTEMPORIZING UPON THE
MUSICAL INSTRUMENT OF HIS INVENTION)

WOULD that the structure brave, the manifold music I
　　build,
　　Bidding my organ obey, calling its keys to their
　　　　work,
Claiming each slave of the sound, at a touch, as when
　　　　Solomon willed
　　Armies of angels that soar, legions of demons that
　　　　lurk,
Man, brute, reptile, fly,—alien of end and of aim,
　　Adverse, each from the other heaven-high, hell-deep
　　　　removed,—
Should rush into sight at once as he named the in-
　　effable Name,
　　And pile him a palace straight, to pleasure the prin-
　　　　cess he loved!

Would it might tarry like his, the beautiful building
　　of mine,
　　This which my keys in a crowd pressed and impor-
　　　　tuned to raise!
Ah, one and all, how they helped, would dispart now
　　　　and now combine,

Zealous to hasten the work, heighten their master
    his praise!
And one would bury his brow with a blind plunge
    down to hell,
  Burrow awhile and build, broad on the roots of
    things,
Then up again swim into sight, having based me my
    palace well,
  Founded it, fearless of flame, flat on the nether
    springs.

And another would mount and march, like the excel-
    lent minion he was,
  Ay, another and yet another, one crowd but with
    many a crest,
Raising my rampired walls of gold as transparent as
    glass,
  Eager to do and die, yield each his place to the rest:
For higher still and higher (as a runner tips with fire,
  When a great illumination surprises a festal night—
Outlined round and round Rome's dome from space to
    spire)
  Up, the pinnacled glory reached, and the pride of
    my soul was in sight.

In sight? Not half! for it seemed, it was certain, to
    match man's birth.

Nature in turn conceived, obeying an impulse as 1;
And the emulous heaven yearned down, made effort to
     reach the earth,
  As the earth had done her best, in my passion, to
     scale the sky:
Novel splendors burst forth, grew familiar and dwelt
     with mine,
  Not a point nor peak but found and fixed its wan-
     dering star;
Meteor-moons, balls of blaze: and they did not pale
     nor pine,
  For earth had attained to heaven, there was no more
     near nor far.

Nay more; for there wanted not who walked in the
     glare and glow,
  Presences plain in the place; or, fresh from the
     Protoplast,
Furnished for ages to come, when a kindlier wind
     should blow,
  Lured now to begin and live, in a house to their
     liking at last;
Or else the wonderful Dead who have passed through
     the body and gone,
  But were back once more to breathe in an old world
     worth their new:

What never had been, was now; what was, as it shall
    be anon;
And what is,—shall I say, matched both? for I was
    made perfect too.

All through my keys that gave their sounds to a wish
    of my soul,
    All through my soul that praised as its wish flowed
        visibly forth,
All through music and me! For think, had I painted
    the whole,
    Why, there it had stood, to see, nor the process so
        wonder-worth:
Had I written the same, made verse—still effect pro-
    ceeds from cause,
    Ye know why the forms are fair, ye hear how the
        tale is told;
It is all triumphant art, but art in obedience to laws,
    Painter and poet are proud in the artist-list en-
        rolled:—

But here is the finger of God, a flash of the will that
    can,
    Existent behind all laws, that made them and, lo,
        they are!
And I know not if, save in this, such gift be allowed
    to man,

That out of three sounds he frame, not a fourth
   sound, but a star,
Consider it well: each tone of our scale in itself is
   naught:
   It is everywhere in the world—loud, soft, and all is
      said:
Give it to me to use! I mix it with two in my thought:
   And there! Ye have heard and seen; consider and
      bow the head!

Well, it is gone at last, the palace of music I reared;
   Gone! and the good tears start, the praises that
      come too siow;
For one is assured at first, one scarce can say that he
      feared,
   That he even gave it a thought, the gone thing was
      to go.
Never to be again! But many more of the kind
   As good, nay, better perchance: is this your comfort
      to me?
To me, who must be saved because I cling with my
      mind
   To the same, same self, same love, same God: ay,
      what was, shall be.

Therefore to whom turn I but to thee, the ineffable
   Name?

Builder and maker, thou, of houses not made with
  hands!
What, have fear of change from thee who art ever the
  same?
  Doubt that thy power can fill the heart that thy
    power expands?
There shall never be one lost good! What was, shall
  live as before;
  The evil is null, is naught, is silence implying sound;
What was good shall be good, with, for evil, so much
    good more;
  On the earth the broken arcs; in the heaven a
    perfect round.

All we have willed or hoped or dreamed of good shall
    exist;
  Not its semblance, but itself; no beauty, nor good,
    nor power
Whose voice has gone forth, but each survives for the
    melodist
  When eternity affirms the conception of an hour.
The high that proved too high, the heroic for earth too
    hard,
  The passion that left the ground to lose itself in the
    sky,
Are music sent up to God by the lover and the bard;

Enough that he heard it once: we shall **hear it by**
and by.

And what is our failure here but a triumph's evidence
For the fulness of the days? Have we withered or
agonized?
Why else was the pause prolonged but that singing
might issue thence?
Why rushed the discords in, but that harmony
should be prized?
Sorrow is hard to bear, and doubt is slow to clear,
Each sufferer says his say, his scheme of the weal
and woe:
But God has a few of us whom he whispers in the
ear;
The rest may reason and welcome: 't is we musi-
cians know.

Well, it is earth with me; silence resumes her reign;
I will be patient and proud, and soberly acquiesce.
Give me the keys. I feel for the common chord again,
Sliding by semitones till I sink to the minor,—yes,
And I blunt it into a ninth, and I stand on alien
ground,
Surveying awhile the heights I rolled from into the
deep;

Which, hark, I have dared and done, for my resting-
    place is found,
  The C Major of this life: so, now I will try to sleep

LYRICS

HOME-THOUGHTS, FROM ABROAD

OH, to be in England
Now that April's there,
And whoever wakes in England
Sees, some morning, unaware,
That the lowest boughs and the brush-wood sheaf
Round the elm-tree bole are in tiny leaf,
While the chaffinch sings on the orchard bough
In England—now!

And after April, when May follows,
And the whitethroat builds, and all the swallows!
Hark, where my blossomed pear-tree in the hedge
Leans to the field and scatters on the clover
Blossoms and dewdrops—at the bent spray's edge—
That's the wise thrush; he sings each song twice over
Lest you should think he never could recapture
The first fine careless rapture!
And though the fields look rough with hoary dew,
And will be gay when noontide wakes anew
The buttercups, the little children's dower
—Far brighter than this gaudy melon-flower!

132

HOME-THOUGHTS, FROM THE SEA

NOBLY, nobly Cape Saint Vincent to the Northwest
    died away;
Sunset ran, one glorious blood-red, reeking into Cadiz
    Bay;
Bluish 'mid the burning water, full in face Trafalgar
    lay;
In the dimmest Northeast distance dawned Gibraltar
    grand and gray;
"Here and here did England help me: how can I help
    England?"—say,
Whoso turns as I, this evening. turn to God to praise
    and pray,
While Jove's planet rises yonder, silent over Africa.

THE LOST LEADER

JUST for a handful of silver he left us,
    Just for a riband to stick in his coat—
Found the one gift of which fortune bereft us,
    Lost all the others she lets us devote;
They, with the gold to give, doled him out silver,
    So much was theirs who so little allowed:
How all our copper had gone for his service!

Rags—were they purple, his heart had been proud!
We that had loved him so, followed him, honored him,
  Lived in his mild and magnificent eye,
Learned his great language, caught his clear accents,
  Made him our pattern to live and to die!
Shakespeare was of us, Milton was for us,
  Burns, Shelley, were with us,—They watch from
    their graves!
He alone breaks from the van and the freemen,
  He alone sinks to the rear and the Slaves'.
We shall march prospering,—not through his presence;
  Songs may inspirit us,—not from his lyre;
Deeds will be done,—while he boasts his quiescence,
  Still bidding crouch whom the rest bade aspire:
Blot out his name, then, record one lost soul more,
  One task more declined, one more footpath untrod,
One more devils-triumph and sorrow for angels,
  One wrong more to man, one more insult to God!
Life's night begins: let him never come back to us!
  There would be doubt, hesitation and pain,
Forced praise on our part—the glimmer of twilight,
  Never glad confident morning again!
Best fight on well, for we taught him—strike gallantly,
  Menace our heart ere we master his own;
Then let him receive the new knowledge and wait us,
  Pardoned in heaven, the first by the throne!

MEMORABILIA

MEMORABILIA

AH, did you once see Shelley plain,
  And did he stop and speak to you,
And did you speak to him again?
  How strange it seems and new!

But you were living before that,
  And also you are living after;
And the memory I started at—
  My starting moves your laughter!

I crossed a moor, with a name of its own
  And a certain use in the world no doubt,
Yet a hand's-breadth of it shines alone
  'Mid the blank miles round about;

For there I picked up on the heather,
  And there I put inside my breast
A moulted feather, an eagle-feather!
  Well, I forget the rest.

MARY WOLLSTONECRAFT AND FUSELI

OH, but is it not hard, Dear?
  Mine are the nerves to quake at a mouse:
If a spider drops I shrink with fear:

I should die outright in a haunted house;
While for you—did the danger dared bring **help**—
From a lion's den I could steal his whelp,
With a serpent round me, stand stock-still,
Go sleep in a churchyard,—so would will
Give me the power to dare and do
Valiantly—just for you!

Much amiss in the head, Dear,
   I toil at a language, tax my brain
Attempting to draw—the scratches here!
   I play, play, practise, and all in vain:
But for you—if my triumph brought you **pride,**
I would grapple with Greek Plays till I died,
Paint a portrait of you—who can tell?
Work my fingers off for your "Pretty well:"
Language and painting and music too,
Easily done—for you!

Strong and fierce in the heart, Dear,
   With—more than a will—what seems **a power**
To pounce on my prey, love outbroke here
   In flame devouring and to devour.
Such love has labored its best and worst
To win me a lover; yet, last as first,
I have not quickened his pulse one **beat,**

Fixed a moment's fancy, bitter or sweet:
Yet the strong fierce heart's love's labor's due,
Utterly lost, was—you!

EVELYN HOPE

BEAUTIFUL Evelyn Hope is dead!
    Sit and watch by her side an hour.
That is her book-shelf, this her bed;
    She plucked that piece of geranium-flower,
Beginning to die too, in the glass;
    Little has yet been changed, I think:
The shutters are shut, no light may pass
    Save two long rays through the hinge's chink.

Sixteen years old when she died!
    Perhaps she had scarcely heard my name;
It was not her time to love; beside,
    Her life had many a hope and aim,
Duties enough and little cares,
    And now was quiet, now astir,
Till God's hand beckoned unawares,—
    And the sweet white brow is all of her.

Is it too late then, Evelyn Hope?
    What, your soul was pure and true,

The good stars met in your horoscope,
  Made you of spirit, fire and dew—
And, just because I was thrice as old
  And our paths in the world diverged so **wide,**
Each was naught to each, must I be told?
  We were fellow mortals, naught beside?

No, indeed! for God above
  Is great to grant, as mighty to make,
And creates the love to reward the love:
  I claim you still, for my own love's sake!
Delayed it may be for more lives yet,
  Through worlds I shall traverse, not a **few:**
Much is to learn, much to forget
  Ere the time be come for taking you.

But the time will come,—at last it will,
  When, Evelyn Hope, what meant (I shall **say)**
In the lower earth, in the years long still,
  That body and soul so pure and gay?
Why your hair was amber, I shall divine,
  And your mouth of your own geranium's **red—**
And what you would do with me, in fine,
  In the new life come in the old one's stead.

I have lived (I shall say) so much since **then,**
  Given up myself so many times,

Gained me the gains of various men,
  Ransacked the ages, spoiled the climes;
Yet one thing, one, in my soul's full scope,
  Either I missed or itself missed me:
And I want and find you, Evelyn Hope!
  What is the issue? let us see!

I loved you, Evelyn, all the while!
  My heart seemed full as it could hold;
There was place and to spare for the frank young
      smile,
  And the red young mouth, and the hair's young gold.
So, hush,—I will give you this leaf to keep;
  See, I shut it inside the sweet cold hand!
There, that is our secret; go to sleep!
  You will wake, and remember, and understand.

LOVE AMONG THE RUINS

WHERE the quiet-colored end of evening smiles
            Miles and miles
On the solitary pastures where our sheep
            Half-asleep
'Tinkle homeward through the twilight, stray or stop
            As they crop—

Was the site once of a city great and gay,
          (So they say)
Of our country's very capital, its prince
          Ages since
Held his court in, gathered councils, wielding **far**
          Peace or war.

Now,—the country does not even boast a tree,
          As you see,
To distinguish slopes of verdure, certain rills
          From the hills
Intersect and give a name to, (else they run
          Into one,)
Where the domed and daring palace shot its spires
          Up like fires
O'er the hundred-gated circuit of a wall
          Bounding all,
Made of marble, men might march on nor be pressed
          Twelve abreast.

And such plenty and perfection, see, of grass
          Never was!
Such a carpet as, this summer-time, o'erspreads
          And embeds
Every vestige of the city, guessed alone,
          Stock or stone—

Where a multitude of men breathed joy and woe
        Long ago;
Lust of glory pricked their hearts up, dread of shame
        Struck them tame;
And that glory and that shame alike, the gold
        Bought and sold.

Now,—the single little turret that remains
        On the plains,
By the caper overrooted, by the gourd
        Overscored,
While the patching houseleek's head of blossom winks
        Through the chinks—
Marks the basement whence a tower in ancient time
        Sprang sublime,
And a burning ring, all round, the chariots traced
        As they raced,
And the monarch and his minions and his dames
        Viewed the games.

And I know, while thus the quiet-colored eve
        Smiles to leave
To their folding, all our many-tinkling fleece
        In such peace,
And the slopes and rills in undistinguished gray
        Melt away—

That a girl with eager eyes and yellow hair
>Waits me there
In the turret whence the charioteers caught soul
>For the goal,
When the king looked, where she looks now, breath-
>less, dumb
>>Till I come.

But he looked upon the city, every side,
>Far and wide,
All the mountains topped with temples, all the glades'
>Colonnades,
All the causeys, bridges, aqueducts,—and then,
>All the men!
When I do come, she will speak not, she will stand,
>Either hand
On my shoulder, give her eyes the first embrace
>Of my face,
Ere we rush, ere we extinguish sight and speech
>Each on each.

In one year they sent a million fighters forth
>South and North,
And they built their gods a brazen pillar high
>As the sky,
Yet reserved a thousand chariots in full force—
>Gold, of course.

Oh heart! oh blood that freezes, blood that **burns!**
          Earth's returns
For whole centuries of folly, noise and sin!
          Shut them in,
With their triumphs and their glories and the **rest!**
          Love is best.

ROMANCES

INCIDENT OF THE FRENCH CAMP

You know, we French stormed Ratisbon:
  A mile or so away,
On a little mound, Napoleon
  Stood on our storming-day;
With neck out-thrust, you fancy how,
  Legs wide, arms locked behind,
As if to balance the prone brow
  Oppressive with its mind.

Just as perhaps he mused "My plans
  That soar, to earth may fall,
Let once my army-leader Lannes
  Waver at yonder wall,"—
Out 'twixt the battery-smokes there flew
  A rider, bound on bound
Full-galloping; nor bridle drew
  Until he reached the mound.

Then off there flung in smiling joy,
  And held himself erect
By just his horse's mane, a boy:
  You hardly could suspect—
(So tight he kept his lips compressed,
  Scarce any blood came through)
You looked twice ere you saw his breast
  Was all but shot in two.

"Well," cried he, "Emperor, by God's grace
  We've got you Ratisbon!
The Marshal 's in the market-place,
  And you'll be there anon
To see your flag-bird flap his vans
  Where I, to heart's desire,
Perched him!" The chief's eye flashed; his plans
  Soared up again like fire.

The chief's eye flashed; but presently
  Softened itself, as sheathes
A film the mother-eagle's eye
  When her bruised eaglet breathes;
"You're wounded!" "Nay," the soldier's pride
  Touched to the quick, he said:
"I'm killed, Sire!" And his chief beside,
  Smiling the boy fell dead.

THE PIED PIPER OF HAMELIN

A CHILD'S STORY

HAMELIN Town 's in Brunswick,
By famous Hanover city;
    The river Weser, deep and wide,
    Washes its wall on the southern side;
    A pleasanter spot you never spied;
But, when begins my ditty,
    Almost five hundred years ago,
    To see the townsfolk suffer so
        From vermin, was a pity.

    Rats!
They fought the dogs and killed the cats,
    And bit the babies in the cradles,
And ate the cheeses out of the vats,
    And licked the soup from the cooks' own ladles,
Split open the kegs of salted sprats,
Made nests inside men's Sunday hats,
And even spoiled the women's chats
    By drowning their speaking
    With shrieking and squeaking
In fifty different sharps and flats.

At last the people in a body
   To the Town Hall came flocking:
" 'T is clear," cried they, "our Mayor 's a noddy;
   And as for our Corporation—shocking
To think we buy gowns lined with ermine
For dolts that can't or won't determine
What 's best to rid us of our vermin!
You hope, because you 're old and obese,
To find in the furry civic robe ease?
Rouse up, sirs! Give your brains a racking
To find the remedy we 're lacking,
Or, sure as fate, we 'll send you packing!"
At this the Mayor and Corporation
Quaked with a mighty consternation.

An hour they sat in council;
   At length the Mayor broke silence:
"For a guilder I 'd my ermine gown sell,
   I wish I were a mile hence!
It 's easy to bid one rack one's brain—
I'm sure my poor head aches again,
I've scratched it so, and all in vain.
Oh for a trap, a trap, a trap!"
Just as he said this, what should hap
At the chamber-door but a gentle tap?

"Bless us," cried the Mayor, "what 's that?
(With the Corporation as he sat,
Looking little though wondrous fat;
Nor brighter was his eye, nor moister
Than a too-long-opened oyster,
Save when at noon his paunch grew mutinous
For a plate of turtle green and glutinous)
"Only a scraping of shoes on the mat?
Anything like the sound of a rat
Makes my heart go pit-a-pat!"

"Come in!"—the Mayor cried, looking bigger
And in did come the strangest figure!
His queer long coat from heel to head
Was half of yellow and half of red,
And he himself was tall and thin,
With sharp blue eyes, each like a pin,
And light loose hair, yet swarthy skin,
No tuft on cheek nor beard on chin,
But lips where smiles went out and in;
There was no guessing his kith and kin:
And nobody could enough admire
The tall man and his quaint attire.
Quoth one: "It 's as my great-grandsire,
Starting up at the Trump of Doom's tone
Had walked this way from his painted tombstone!"

He advanced to the council-table:
And, "Please your honors," said he, "I'm able,
By means of a secret charm, to draw
All creatures living beneath the sun,
That creep or swim or fly or run,
After me so as you never saw!
And I chiefly use my charm
On creatures that do people harm,
The mole and toad and newt and viper;
And people call me the Pied Piper."
(And here they noticed round his neck
A scarf of red and yellow stripe,
To match with his coat of the self-same cheque;
And at the scarf's end hung a pipe;
And his fingers, they noticed, were ever straying
As if impatient to be playing
Upon this pipe, as low it dangled
Over his vesture so old-fangled.)
"Yet," said he, "poor piper as I am,
In Tartary I freed the Cham,
Last June, from his huge swarms of gnats;
I eased in Asia the Nizam
Of a monstrous brood of vampire-bats:
And as for what your brain bewilders,
If I can rid your town of rats
Will you give me a thousand guilders?'"

"One? fifty thousand!"—was the exclamation
Of the astonished Mayor and Corporation.

Into the street the Piper stept,
  Smiling first a little smile,
As if he knew what magic slept
  In his quiet pipe the while;
Then, like a musical adept,
To blow the pipe his lips he wrinkled,
And green and blue his sharp eyes twinkled,
Like a candle-flame where salt is sprinkled;
And ere three shrill notes the pipe uttered,
You heard as if an army muttered;
And the muttering grew to a grumbling;
And the grumbling grew to a mighty rumbling;
And out of the houses the rats came tumbling.
Great rats, small rats, lean rats, brawny rats,
Brown rats, black rats, gray rats, tawny rats,
Grave old plodders, gay young friskers,
  Fathers, mothers, uncles, cousins,
Cocking tails and pricking whiskers,
  Families by tens and dozens,
Brothers, sisters, husbands, wives—
Followed the Piper for their lives.
From street to street he piped advancing,
And step for step they followed dancing,

Until they came to the river Weser,
Wherein all plunged and perished!
—Save one who, stout as Julius Cæsar,
Swam across and lived to carry
(As he, the manuscript he cherished)
To Rat-land home his commentary:
Which was, "At the first shrill notes of the pipe,
I heard a sound as of scraping tripe,
And putting apples, wondrous ripe,
Into a cider-press's gripe:
And a moving away of pickle-tub-boards,
And a leaving ajar of conserve-cupboards,
And a drawing the corks of train-oil-flasks,
And a breaking the hoops of butter-casks:
And it seemed as if a voice
(Sweeter far than by harp or by psaltery
Is breathed) called out, 'Oh rats, rejoice!
The world is grown to one vast drysaltery!
So munch on, crunch on, take your nuncheon,
Breakfast, supper, dinner, luncheon!'
And just as a bulky sugar-puncheon,
All ready staved, like a great sun shone
Glorious scarce an inch before me,
Just as methought it said, 'Come, bore me!'
—I found the Weser rolling o'er me."

You should have heard the Hamelin people
Ringing the bells till they rocked the steeple.
"Go," cried the Mayor, "and get long poles,
Poke out the nests and block up the holes!
Consult with carpenters and builders,
And leave in our town not even a trace
Of the rats!"—when suddenly, up the face
Of the Piper perked in the market-place,
With a, "First, if you please, my thousand
      guilders!"

A thousand guilders! The Mayor looked blue;
So did the Corporation too.
For council dinners made rare havoc
With Claret, Moselle, Vin-de-Grave, Hock;
And half the money would replenish
Their cellar's biggest butt with Rhenish.
To pay this sum to a wandering fellow
With a gypsy coat of red and yellow!
"Beside," quoth the Mayor with a knowing wink,
"Our business was done at the river's brink;
We saw with our eyes the vermin sink,
And what 's dead can't come to life, I think.
So, friend, we 're not the folks to shrink
From the duty of giving you something for drink,
And a matter of money to put in your poke;

But as for the guilders, what we spoke
Of them, as you very well know, was in joke.
Beside, our losses have made us thrifty.
A thousand guilders! Come, take fifty!"

The Piper's face fell, and he cried,
"No trifling! I can't wait, beside!
I've promised to visit by dinner time
Bagdat, and accept the prime
Of the Head-Cook's pottage, all he 's rich in,
For having left, in the Caliph's kitchen,
Of a nest of scorpions no survivor:
With him I proved no bargain-driver,
With you, don't think I 'll bate a stiver!
And folks who put me in a passion
May find me pipe after another fashion."
"How?" cried the Mayor, "d' ye think I brook
Being worse treated than a Cook?
Insulted by a lazy ribald
With idle pipe and vesture piebald?
You threaten us, fellow? Do your worst,
Blow your pipe there till you burst!"

Once more he stept into the street,
    And to his lips again
Laid his long pipe of smooth straight cane;
    And ere he blew three notes (such sweet

Soft notes as yet musician's cunning
  Never gave the enraptured air)
There was a rustling that seemed like a bustling
Of merry crowds justling at pitching and hustling;
Small feet were pattering, wooden shoes clattering,
Little hands clapping and little tongues chattering,
And, like fowls in a farm-yard when barley is
     scattering,
Out came the children running.
All the little boys and girls,
With rosy cheeks and flaxen curls,
And sparkling eyes and teeth like pearls,
Tripping and skipping, ran merrily after
The wonderful music with shouting and laughter.

The Mayor was dumb, and the Council stood
As if they were changed into blocks of wood,
Unable to move a step, or cry
To the children merrily skipping by,
—Could only follow with the eye
That joyous crowd at the Piper's back.
But how the Mayor was on the rack,
And the wretched Council's bosoms beat,
As the Piper turned from the High Street
To where the Weser rolled its waters
Right in the way of their sons and daughters!

However, he turned from South to West,
And to Koppelberg Hill his steps addressed,
And after him the children pressed;
Great was the joy in every breast.
"He never can cross that mighty top!
He 's forced to let the piping drop,
And we shall see our children stop!"
When, lo, as they reached the mountain-side,
A wondrous portal opened wide,
As if a cavern was suddenly hollowed;
And the Piper advanced and the children followed,
And when all were in to the very last,
The door in the mountain-side shut fast.
Did I say, all? No! One was lame,
And could not dance the whole of the way;
And in after years, if you would blame
His sadness, he was used to say,—
"It's dull in our town since my playmates left!
I can't forget that I'm bereft
Of all the pleasant sights they see,
Which the Piper also promised me.
For he led us, he said, to a joyous land,
Joining the town and just at hand,
Where waters gushed and fruit-trees grew
And flowers put forth a fairer hue,
And everything was strange and new;

The sparrows were brighter than peacocks here,
And their dogs outran our fallow deer,
And honey-bees had lost their stings,
And horses were born with eagles' wings:
And just as I became assured
My lame foot would be speedily cured,
The music stopped and I stood still,
And found myself outside the hill,
Left alone against my will,
To go now limping as before,
And never hear of that country more!"

Alas, alas for Hamelin!
   There came into many a burgher's pate
   A text which says that heaven's gate
   Opes to the rich at as easy rate
As the needle's eye takes a camel in!
The Mayor sent East, West, North and South,
To offer the Piper, by word of mouth,
   Wherever it was men's lot to find him,
Silver and gold to his heart's content,
If he'd only return the way he went,
   And bring the children behind him.
But when they saw 't was a lost endeavor,
And Piper and dancers were gone forever,
They made a decree that lawyers never

Should think their records dated duly
If, after the day of the month and year,
These words did not as well appear,
"And so long after what happened here
  On the Twenty-second of July,
Thirteen hundred and seventy-six:"
And the better in memory to fix
The place of the children's last retreat,
They called it, the Pied Piper's Street—
Where any one playing on pipe or tabor
Was sure for the future to lose his labor.
Nor suffered they hostelry or tavern

  To shock with mirth a street so solemn;
But opposite the place of the cavern

  They wrote the story on a column,
And on the great church-window painted
The same, to make the world acquainted
How their children were stolen away,
And there it stands to this very day.
And I must not omit to say
That in Transylvania there 's a tribe
Of alien people who ascribe
The outlandish ways and dress
On which their neighbors lay such stress,
To their fathers and mothers having risen
Out of some subterraneous prison

Into which they were trepanned.
Long time ago in a mighty band
Out of Hamelin town in Brunswick land,
But how or why, they don't understand.

So, Willy, let me and you be wipers
Of scores out with all men—especially pipers!
And, whether they pipe us free fróm rats or fróm
      mice,
If we 've promised them aught, let us keep our
      promise!

THE BOY AND THE ANGEL

Morning, evening, noon and night,
"Praise God!" sang Theocrite.

Then to his poor trade he turned,
Whereby the daily meal was earned.

Hard he labored, long and well:
O'er his work the boy's curls fell.

But ever, at each period,
He stopped and sang, "Praise God!"

Then back again his curls he threw,
And cheerful turned to work anew.

Said Blaise, the listening monk, "Well done:
I doubt not thou art heard, my son:

"As well as if thy voice to-day
Were praising God, the Pope's great way.

"This Easter Day, the Pope at Rome
Praises God from Peter's dome."

Said Theocrite, "Would God that I
Might praise him that great way, and die!"

Night passed, day shone,
And Theocrite was gone.

With God a day endures alway,
A thousand years are but a day.

God said in heaven, "Nor day nor night
Now brings the voice of my delight."

Then Gabriel, like a rainbow's birth,
Spread his wings and sank to earth;

Entered, in flesh, the empty cell,
Lived there, and played the craftsman well:

And morning, evening, noon and night,
Praised God in place of Theocrite.

And from a boy, to youth he grew:
The man put off the stripling's hue:

The man matured and fell away
Into the season of decay:

And ever o'er the trade he bent,
And ever lived on earth content.

(He did God's will; to him, all one
If on the earth or in the sun.)

God said, "A praise is in mine ear;
There is no doubt in it, no fear:

"So sing old worlds, and so
New worlds that from my footstool go.

"Clearer loves sound other ways:
I miss my little human praise."

Then forth sprang Gabriel's wings, off fell
The flesh disguise, remained the cell.

'T was Easter Day: he flew to Rome,
And paused above Saint Peter's dome.

In the tiring-room close by
The great outer gallery,

With his holy vestments dight,
Stood the new Pope, Theocrite:

And all his past career
Came back upon him clear,

Since when, a boy, he plied his trade,
Till on his life the sickness weighed;

And in his cell, when death drew near,
An angel in a dream brought cheer:

And rising from the sickness drear,
He grew a priest, and now stood here.

To the East with praise he turned,
And on his sight the angel burned.

"I bore thee from thy craftsman's cell,
And set thee here; I did not well.

"Vainly I left my angel-sphere,
Vain was thy dream of many a year.

"Thy voice's praise seemed weak; it dropped—
Creation's chorus stopped!

"Go back and praise again
The early way, while I remain.

"With that weak voice of our disdain,
Take up creation's pausing strain.

"Back to the cell and poor employ:
Resume the craftsman and the boy!"

Theocrite grew old at home;
A new Pope dwelt in Peter's dome.

One vanished as the other died:
They sought God side by side.

THE STATUE AND THE BUST

THERE 's a palace in Florence, the world knows well,
And a statue watches it from the square,
And this story of both do our townsmen tell.
Ages ago, a lady there,
At the farthest window facing the East
Asked, "Who rides by with the royal air?"

The bridesmaids' prattle around her ceased;
She leaned forth, one on either hand;
They saw how the blush of the bride increased—
They felt by its beats her heart expand—
As one at each ear and both in a breath
Whispered, "The Great-Duke Ferdinand."

That selfsame instant, underneath,
The Duke rode past in his idle way,
Empty and fine like a swordless sheath.
Gay he rode, with a friend as gay,
Till he threw his head back—"Who is she?"
—"A bride the Riccardi brings home to-day."

Hair in heaps lay heavily
Over a pale brow spirit-pure—
Carved like the heart of the coal-black tree,
Crisped like a war-steed's encolure—
And vainly sought to dissemble her eyes
Of the blackest black our eyes endure,

And lo, a blade for a knight's emprise
Filled the fine empty sheath of a man,—
The Duke grew straightway brave and wise.
He looked at her, as a lover can;
She looked at him, as one who awakes:
The past was a sleep, and her life began.

Now, love so ordered for both their sakes,
A feast was held that selfsame night
In the pile which the mighty shadow makes.
(For Via Larga is three-parts light,
But the palace overshadows one,
Because of a crime, which may God requite!

To Florence and God the wrong was done,
Through the first republic's murder there
By Cosimo and his cursed son.)
The Duke (with the statue's face in the square)
Turned in the midst of his multitude
At the bright approach of the bridal pair.

Face to face the lovers stood
A single minute and no more,
While the bridegroom bent as a man subdued—
Bowed till his bonnet brushed the floor—
For the Duke on the lady a kiss conferred,
As the courtly custom was of yore.

In a minute can lovers exchange a word?
If a word did pass, which I do not think,
Only one out of a thousand heard.
That was the bridegroom. At day's brink
He and his bride were alone at last
In a bed chamber by a taper's blink.

Calmly he said that her lot was cast,
That the door she had passed was shut on her
Till the final catafalk repassed.
The world meanwhile, its noise and stir,
Through a certain window facing the East
She could watch like a convent's chronicler.

Since passing the door might lead to a feast,
And a feast might lead to so much beside,
He, of many evils, chose the least.
"Freely I choose too," said the bride—
"Your window and its world suffice,"
Replied the tongue, while the heart replied—

"If I spend the night with that devil twice,
May his window serve as my loop of hell
Whence a damned soul looks on paradise!
I fly to the Duke who loves me well,
Sit by his side and laugh at sorrow
Ere I count another ave-bell.

" 'T is only the coat of a page to borrow.
And tie my hair in a horse-boy's trim.
And I save my soul—but not to-morrow"—
(She checked herself and her eye grew dim)
"My father tarries to bless my state:
I must keep it one day more for him.

"Is one day more so long to wait?
Moreover the Duke rides past, I know;
We shall see each other, sure as fate."
She turned on her side and slept. Just so!
So we resolve on a thing and sleep:
So did the lady, ages ago.

That night the Duke said, "Dear or cheap
As the cost of this cup of bliss may prove
To body or soul, I will drain it deep."
And on the morrow, bold with love,
He beckoned the bridegroom (close on call,
As his duty bade, by the Duke's alcove)

And smiled " 'T was a very funeral,
Your lady will think, this feast of ours,—
A shame to efface, whate'er befall!
What if we break from the Arno bowers,
And try Petraja, cool and green,
Cure last night's fault with this morning's flowers?"

The bridegroom, not a thought to be seen
On his steady brow and quiet mouth,
Said, "Too much favor for me so mean!
But, alas! my lady leaves the South;
Each wind that comes from the Apennine
Is a menace to her tender youth:

"Nor a way exists, the wise opine,
If she quits her palace twice this year,
To avert the flower of life's decline."
Quoth the Duke, "A sage and a kindly fear.
Moreover Petraja is cold this spring:
Be our feast to-night as usual here!"

And then to himself—"Which night shall bring
Thy bride to her lover's embraces, fool—
Or I am the fool, and thou art the king!
Yet my passion must wait a night, nor cool—
For to-night the Envoy arrives from France
Whose heart I unlock with thyself, my tool.

"I need thee still and might miss perchance.
To-day is not wholly lost, beside,
With its hope of my lady's countenance:
For I ride—what should I do but ride?
And passing her palace, if I list,
May glance at its window—well betide!"

So said, so done: nor the lady missed
One ray that broke from the ardent brow,
Nor a curl of the lips where the spirit kissed.
Be sure that each renewed the vow
No morrow's sun should arise and set
And leave them then as it left them now.

But next day passed, and next day yet,
With still fresh cause to wait one day more
Ere each leaped over the parapet.
And still, as love's brief morning wore,
With a gentle start, half smile, half sigh,
They found love not as it seemed before.

They thought it would work infallibly,
But not in despite of heaven and earth:
The rose would blow when the storm passed by
Meantime they could profit in winter's dearth
By store of fruits that supplant the rose:
The world and its ways have a certain worth:

And to press a point while these oppose
Were simple policy; better wait:
We lose no friends and we gain no foes.
Meantime, worse fates than a lover's fate,
Who daily may ride and pass and look
Where his lady watches behind the grate!

And she—she watched the square like a book
Holding one picture and only one,
Which daily to find she undertook:
When the picture was reached the book was done
And she turned from the picture at night to scheme
Of tearing it out for herself next sun.

So weeks grew months, years; gleam by gleam
The glory dropped from their youth and love,
And both perceived they had dreamed a dream;
Which hovered as dreams do, still above:
But who can take a dream for a truth?
Oh, hide our eyes from the next remove!

One day as the lady saw her youth
Depart, and the silver thread that streaked
Her hair, and, worn by the serpent's tooth,
The brow so puckered, the chin so peaked,—
And wondered who the woman was,
Hollow-eyed and haggard-cheeked,

Fronting her silent in the glass—
"Summon here," she suddenly said,
"Before the rest of my old self pass,
Him, the Carver, a hand to aid,
Who fashions the clay no love will change,
And fixes a beauty never to fade.

"Let Robbia's craft so apt and strange
Arrest the remains of young and fair,
And rivet them while the seasons range.
Makes me a face on the window there,
Waiting as ever, mute the while,
My love to pass below in the square!

"And let me think that it may beguile
Dreary days which the dead must spend
Down in their darkness under the aisle,
To say, 'What matters it at the end?
I did no more while my heart was warm
Than does that image, my pale-faced friend.'

"Where is the use of the lip's red charm,
The heaven of hair, the pride of the brow,
And the blood that blues the inside arm—
Unless we turn, as the soul knows how,
The earthly gift to an end divine?
A lady of clay is as good, I trow."

But long ere Robbia's cornice, fine,
With flowers and fruits which leaves enlace,
Was set where now is the empty shrine—
(And leaning out of a bright blue space,
As a ghost might lean from a chink of sky,
The passionate pale lady's face—

Eying ever, with earnest eye
And quick-turned neck at its breathless stretch
Some one who ever is passing by—)
The Duke had sighed like the simplest wretch
In Florence, "Youth—my dream escapes!
Will its record stay?" And he bade them fetch

Some subtle moulder of brazen shapes—
"Can the soul, the will, die out of a man
Ere his body find the grave that gapes?
John of Douay shall effect my plan

Set me on horseback here aloft,
Alive, as the crafty sculptor can,

"In the very square I have crossed so oft:
That men may admire, when future suns
Shall touch the eyes to a purpose soft.
While the mouth and the brow stay brave in bronze—
Admire and say, 'When he was alive
How he would take his pleasure once!"

"And it shall go hard but I contrive
To listen the while, and laugh in my tomb
At idleness which aspires to strive."

———

So! While these wait the trump of doom,
How do their spirits pass, I wonder,
Nights and days in the narrow room?

Still, I suppose, they sit and ponder
What a gift life was, ages ago,
Six steps out of the chapel yonder.
Only they see not God, I know,
Nor all that chivalry of his,
The soldier-saints who, row on row,

Burn upward each to his point of bliss—
Since, the end of life being manifest,
He had burned his way through the world to this.
I hear you reproach, "But delay was best,
For their end was a crime."—Oh, a crime will do
As well, I reply, to serve for a test,

As a virtue golden through and through,
Sufficient to vindicate itself
And prove its worth at a moment's view!
Must a game be played for the sake of pelf?
Where a button goes, 't were an epigram
To offer the stamp of the very Guelph.

The true has no value beyond the sham:
As well the counter as coin, I submit,
When your table 's a hat, and your prize, a dram
Stake your counter as boldly every whit,
Venture as warily, use the same skill,
Do your best, whether winning or losing it.

If you choose to play!—is my principle.
Let a man contend to the uttermost
For his life's set prize, be it what it will!
The counter our lovers staked was lost
As surely as if it were lawful coin:
And the sin I impute to each frustrate ghost

Is—the unlit lamp and the ungirt loin,
Though the end in sight was a vice, I say.
You of the virtue (we issue join)
How strive you?   *De te, fabula!*

DRAMA

PIPPA PASSES

PERSONS

PIPPA.	JULES.
OTTIMA.	PHENE.
SEBALD.	Austrian Police.
Foreign Students.	BLUPHOCKS.
GOTTLIEB.	LUIGI and his mother.
SCHRAMM.	Poor Girls.

MONSIGNOR and his attendants.

INTRODUCTION

NEW YEAR'S DAY AT ASOLO IN THE TREVISAN

A large mean airy chamber. A girl, PIPPA, *from the
silk-mills, springing out of bed.*

DAY!
Faster and more fast,
O'er night's brim, day boils at last:
Boils, pure gold, o'er the cloud-cup's **brim**
Where spurting and suppressed it **lay,**

For not a froth-flake touched the rim
Of yonder gap in the solid gray
Of the eastern cloud, an hour away;
But forth one wavelet, then another, curled,
Till the whole sunrise, not to be suppressed,
Rose, reddened, and its seething breast
Flickered in bounds, grew gold, then overflowed the
        world

Oh Day, if I squander a wavelet of thee,
A mite of my twelve-hours' treasure,
The least of thy gazes or glances,
(Be they grants thou art bound to or gifts above
        measure)
One of thy choices or one of thy chances,
(Be they tasks God imposed thee or freaks at thy
        pleasure)
—My Day, if I squander such labor or leisure,
Then shame fall on Asolo, mischief on me!

Thy long blue solemn hours serenely flowing,
Whence earth, we feel, gets steady help and good—
Thy fitful sunshine-minutes, coming, going,
As if earth turned from work in gamesome mood—
All shall be mine! But thou must treat me not
As prosperous ones are treated, those who live
At hand here, and enjoy the higher lot,
In readiness to take what thou wilt give

And free to let alone what thou refusest;
For, Day, my holiday, if thou ill-usest
Me, who am only Pippa,—old-year's sorrow,
Cast off last night, will come again to-morrow:
Whereas, if thou prove gentle, I shall borrow
Sufficient strength of thee for new-year's sorrow.
All other men and women that this earth
Belongs to, who all days alike possess,
Make general plenty cure particular dearth,
Get more joy one way, if another, less:
Thou art my single day, God lends to leaven
What were all earth else, with a feel of heaven,—
Sole light that helps me through the year, thy sun's!
Try now! Take Asolo's Four Happiest Ones—
And let thy morning rain on that superb
Great haughty Ottima; can rain disturb
Her Sebald's homage? All the while thy rain
Beats fiercest on her shrub-house window-pane
He will but press the closer, breathe more warm
Against her cheek; how should she mind the storm?
And, morning past, if mid-day shed a gloom
O'er Jules and Phene,—what care bride and groom
Save for their dear selves? 'Tis their marriage-day;
And while they leave church and go home their way,
Hand clasping hand, within each breast would be
Sunbeams and pleasant weather spite of thee.
Then, for another trial obscure thy eve

With mist,—will Luigi and his mother grieve—
The lady and her child, unmatched, forsooth,
She in her age, as Luigi in his youth,
For true content? The cheerful town, warm, close
And safe, the sooner that thou art morose,
Receives them. And yet once again, outbreak
In storm at night on Monsignor, they make
Such stir about,—whom they expect from Rome
To visit Asolo, his brothers' home,
And say here masses proper to release
A soul from pain,—what storm dares hurt his peace?
Calm would he pray, with his own thoughts to ward
Thy thunder off, nor want the angels' guard.
But Pippa—just one such mischance would spoil
Her day that lightens the next twelvemonth's toil
At wearisome silk-winding, coil on coil!

   And here I let time slip for naught!
Aha, you foolhardy sunbeam, caught
With a single splash from my ewer!
You that would mock the best pursuer,
Was my basin over-deep?
One splash of water ruins you asleep,
And up, up, fleet your brilliant bits
Wheeling and counterwheeling,
Reeling, broken beyond healing:
Now grow together on the ceiling!
That will task your wits.

Whoever it was quenched fire first, hoped to see
Morsel after morsel flee
As merrily, as giddily . . .
Meantime, what lights my sunbeam on,
Where settles by degrees the radiant cripple?
Oh, is it surely blown, my martagon?
New-blown and ruddy as St. Agnes' nipple,
Plump as the flesh-bunch on some Turk bird's poll!
Be sure if corals, branching 'neath the ripple
Of ocean, bud there,—fairies watch unroll
Such turban-flowers; I say, such lamps disperse
Thick red flame through that dusk green universe!
I am queen of thee, floweret!
And each fleshy blossom
Preserve I not—(safer
Than leaves that embower it,
Or shells that embosom)
—From weevil and chafer?
Laugh through my pane then; solicit the bee;
Gibe him, be sure; and, in midst of thy glee,
Love thy queen, worship me!

—Worship whom else? For am I not, this day,
Whate'er I please? What shall I please to-day?
My morn, noon, eve and night—how spend my day?
To-morrow I must be Pippa who winds silk,
The whole year round, to earn just bread and milk;

But, this one day, I have leave to go,
And play out my fancy's fullest games;
I may fancy all day—and it shall be so—
That I taste of the pleasures, am called by the names
Of the Happiest Four in our Asolo!

See! Up the hillside yonder, through the morning,
Some one shall love me, as the world calls love:
I am no less than Ottima, take warning!
The gardens, and the great stone house above,
And other house for shrubs, all glass in front,
Are mine; where Sebald steals, as he is wont,
To court me, while old Luca yet reposes:
And therefore, till the shrub-house door uncloses,
I . . . what now?—give abundant cause for prate
About me—Ottima, I mean—of late,
Too bold, too confident she 'll still face down
The spitefullest of talkers in our town.
How we talk in the little town below!
    But love, love, love—there 's better love, I know!
This foolish love was only day's first offer;
I choose my next love to defy the scoffer:
For do not our Bride and Bridegroom sally
Out of Possagno church at noon?
Their house looks over Orcana valley:
Why should not I be the bride as soon
As Ottima? For I saw, beside,

Arrive last night that little bride—
Saw, if you call it seeing her, one flash
Of the pale snow-pure cheek and black bright tresses,
Blacker than all except the black eyelash;
I wonder she contrives those lids no dresses!
—So strict was she, the veil
Should cover close her pale
Pure cheeks—a bride to look at and scarce touch,
Scarce touch, remember, Jules!   For are not such
Used to be tended, flower-like, every feature,
As if one's breath would fray the lily of a creature?
A soft and easy life these ladies lead:
Whiteness in us were wonderful indeed.
Oh, save that brow its virgin dimness,
Keep that foot its lady primness,
Let those ankles never swerve
From their exquisite reserve,
Yet have to trip along the streets like me,
All but naked to the knee!
How will she ever grant her Jules a bliss
So startling as her real first infant kiss?
Oh, no—not envy, this!

—Not envy, sure!—for if you gave me
Leave to take or to refuse,
In earnest, do you think I 'd choose
That sort of new love to enslave me?

Mine should have lapped me round from the begin-
    ning;
As little fear of losing it as winning:
Lovers grow cold, men learn to hate their wives,
And only parents' love can last our lives.
At eve the Son and Mother, gentle pair,
Commune inside our turret: what prevents
My being Luigi? While that mossy lair
Of lizards through the winter-time is stirred
With each to each imparting sweet intents
For this new-year, as brooding bird to bird—
(For I observe of late, the evening walk
Of Luigi and his mother, always ends
Inside our ruined turret, where they talk,
Calmer than lovers, yet more kind than friends)
—Let me be cared about, kept out of harm,
And schemed for, safe in love as with a charm;
Let me be Luigi! If I only knew
What was my mother's face—my father, too!
    Nay, if you come to that, best love of all
Is God's; then why not have God's love befall
Myself as, in the palace by the Dome,
Monsignor?—who to-night will bless the home
Of his dead brother; and God bless in turn
That heart which beats, those eyes which mildly burn
With love for all men! I, to-night at least,
Would be that holy and beloved priest.

Now wait!—even I already seem to share
In God's love: what does New-year's hymn declare?
What other meaning do these verses bear?

> *All service ranks the same with God:*
> *If now, as formerly he trod*
> *Paradise, his presence fills*
> *Our earth, each only as God wills*
> *Can work—God's puppets, best and worst,*
> *Are we; there is no last nor first.*
>
> *Say not "a small event!" Why "small"?*
> *Costs it more pain that this, ye call*
> *A "great event," should come to pass,*
> *Than that? Untwine me from the mass*
> *Of deeds which make up life, one deed*
> *Power shall fall short in or exceed!*

And more of it, and more of it!—oh yes—
I will pass each, and see their happiness,
And envy none—being just as great, no doubt,
Useful to men, and dear to God, as they!
A pretty thing to care about
So mightily, this single holiday!
But let the sun shine! Wherefore repine?
—With thee to lead me, O Day of mine,
Down the grass path gray with dew,
Under the pine-wood, blind with boughs,

Where the swallow never flew
Nor yet cicala dared carouse—
No, dared carouse!   [*She enters the street.*

I. MORNING

Up the Hillside, inside the Shrub-house. LUCA's *Wife,*
  OTTIMA, *and her Paramour, the German* SEBALD.

Sebald. [*sings.*] *Let the watching lids wink!*
                     Day's ablaze with eyes, think!
                     Deep into the night, drink!
  Ottima.   Night?   Such may be your Rhineland
       nights, perhaps;
But this blood-red beam through the shutter's chink
—We call such light, the morning: let us see!
Mind how you grope your way, though! How these
       tall
Naked geraniums straggle! Push the lattice
Behind that frame!—Nay, do I bid you?—Sebald,
It shakes the dust down on me! Why, of course
The slide-bolt catches. Well, are you content,
Or must I find you something else to spoil?
Kiss and be friends, my Sebald! Is 't full morning?
Oh, don't speak then!
  Seb.   Ay, thus it used to be!
Ever your house was, I remember, shut
'Till mid-day; I observed that, as I strolled

On mornings through the vale here; country girls
Were noisy, washing garments in the brook,
Hinds drove the slow white oxen up the hills:
But no, your house was mute, would ope no eye!
And wisely: you were plotting one thing there,
Nature, another outside. I looked up—
Rough white wood shutters, rusty iron bars,
Silent as death, blind in a flood of light.
Oh, I remember!—and the peasants laughed
And said, "The old man sleeps with the young wife."
This house was his, this chair, this window—his.

   Otti. Ah, the clear morning! I can see Saint Mark's;
That black streak is the belfry. Stop: Vicenza
Should lie . . . there 's Padua, plain enough, that
      blue!
Look o'er my shoulder, follow my finger!
   Seb.   Morning?
It seems to me a night with a sun added.
Where 's dew, where 's freshness? That bruised plant,
      I bruised
In getting through the lattice yestereve,
Droops as it did. See, here's my elbow's mark
I' the dust o' the sill.
   Otti.   Oh, shut the lattice, pray!
   Seb. Let me lean out. I cannot scent blood here,
Foul as the morn may be.
               There, shut the world out!

How do you feel now, Ottima?   There, curse
The world and all outside!   Let us throw off
This mask: how do you bear yourself?   Let's out
With all of it!

    Ott.   Best never speak of it.

    Seb.   Best speak again and yet again of it,
'Till words cease to be more than words.   "His blood."
For instance—let those two words mean, "His blood"
And nothing more.   Notice, I'll say them now,
"His blood."

    Otti.   Assuredly if I repented
The deed—

    Seb.   Repent?   Who should repent, or why?
What puts that in your head?   Did I once say
That I repented?

    Otti.   No; I said the deed . . .

    Seb.   "The deed" and "the event"—just now it was
"Our passion's fruit"—the devil take such cant!
Say, once and always, Luca was a wittol,
I am his cut-throat, you are . . .

    Otti.   Here's the wine;
I brought it when we left the house above,
And glasses too—wine of both sorts.   Black?   White
      then?

    Seb.   But am not I his cut-throat?   What are you?

    Otti.   There trudges on his business from the Duomo
Benet the Capuchin, with his brown hood

And bare feet; always in one place at church
Close under the stone wall by the south entry.
I used to take him for a brown cold piece
Of the wall's self, as out of it he rose
To let me pass—at first, I say, I used:
Now, so has that dumb figure fastened on me,
I rather should account the plastered wall
A piece of him, so chilly does it strike.
This, Sebald?

   Seb. No, the white wine—the white wine!
Well, Ottima, I promised no new year
Should rise on us the ancient shameful way;
Nor does it rise. Pour on! To your black eyes!
Do you remember last damned New Year's day?

   Otti. You brought those foreign prints. We looked
      at them
Over the wine and fruit. I had to scheme
To get him from the fire. Nothing but saying
His own set wants the proof-mark, roused him up
To hunt them out.

   Seb.   'Faith, he is not alive
To fondle you before my face.

   Otti.   Do you
Fondle me then! Who means to take your life
For that, my Sebald?

   Seb.   Hark you, Ottima!
One thing to guard against. We 'll not make much

One of the other—that is, not make more
Parade of warmth, childish officious coil,
Than yesterday: as if, sweet, I supposed
Proof upon proof were needed now, now first,
To show I love you—yes, still love you—love you
In spite of Luca and what's come to him
—Sure sign we had him ever in our thoughts,
White sneering old reproachful face and all!
We 'll even quarrel, love, at times, as if
We still could lose each other, were not tied
By this: conceive you?

   Otti.   Love!

   Seb.   Not tied so sure!
Because though I was wrought upon, have struck
His insolence back into him—am I
So surely yours?—therefore forever yours?

   Otti.   Love, to be wise, (one counsel pays another,)
Should we have—months ago, when first we loved,
For instance that May morning we two stole
Under the green ascent of sycamores—
If we had come upon a thing like that
Suddenly . . .

   Seb.   "A thing"—there again—"a thing!"

   Otti.   Then, Venus' body, had we come upon
My husband Luca Gaddi's murdered corpse
Within there, at his couch-foot, covered close—
Would you have pored upon it? Why persist

In poring now upon it? For 't is here
As much as there in the deserted house:
You cannot rid your eyes of it. For me,
Now he is dead I hate him worse: I hate . . .
Dare you stay here? I would go back and hold
His two dead hands, and say, "I hate you worse,
Luca, than" . . .

   Seb. Off, off—take your hands off mine,
'T is the hot evening—off! oh, morning is it?

    Otti. There 's one thing must be done; you know
        what thing.

Come in and help to carry. We may sleep
Anywhere in the whole wide house to-night.

    Seb. What would come, think you, if we let him
        lie

Just as he is? Let him lie there until
The angels take him! He is turned by this
Off from his face beside, as you will see.

    Otti. This dusty pane might serve for looking-
        glass.

A plait of hair should wave across my neck?
Three, four—four gray hairs! Is it so you said
A plait of hair should wave across my neck?
No—this way.

    Seb.   Ottima, I would give your neck,
Each splendid shoulder, both those breasts of yours,
That this were undone! Killing! Kill the world,

So Luca lives again!—ay, lives to sputter
His fulsome dotage on you—yes, and feign
Surprise that I return at eve to sup,
When all the morning I was loitering here—
Bid me dispatch my business and begone.
I would . . .

    Otti.   See!

    Seb.   No, I'll finish. Do you think
I fear to speak the bare truth once for all?
All we have talked of, is, at bottom, fine
To suffer; there 's a recompense in guilt;
One must be venturous and fortunate:
What is one young for, else? In age we 'll sigh
O'er the wild reckless wicked days flown over;
Still, we have lived: the vice was in its place.
But to have eaten Luca's bread, have worn
His clothes, have felt his money swell my purse—
Do lovers in romances sin that way?
Why, I was starving when I used to call
And teach you music, starving while you plucked me
These flowers to smell!

    Otti.   My poor lost friend!

    Seb.   He gave me
Life, nothing less: what if he did reproach
My perfidy, and threaten, and do more—
Had he no right? What was to wonder at?
He sat by us at table quietly:

Why must you lean across till our cheeks touched?
Could he do less than make pretence to strike?
'T is not the crime's sake—I'd commit ten crimes
Greater, to have this crime wiped out, undone!
And you—O how feel you? Feel you for me?

   Otti. Well then, I love you better now than **ever,**
And best (look at me while I speak to you)—
Best for the crime; nor do I grieve, in truth,
This mask, this simulated ignorance,
This affectation of simplicity,
Falls off our crime; this naked crime of ours
May not now be looked over: look it down!
Great? let it be great; but the joys it brought,
Pay they or no its price? Come: they or it!
Speak not! The past, would you give up the past
Such as it is, pleasure and crime together?
Give up that noon I owned my love for **you?**
The garden's silence: even the single bee
Persisting in his toil, suddenly stopped,
And where he hid you only could surmise
By some campanula chalice set a-swing.
Who stammered—"Yes, I love you?"

   Seb.   **And I drew**
Back; put far back your face with both my hands
Lest you should grow too full of me—your face
So seemed athirst for my whole soul and body!

Otti.   And when I ventured to receive you here,
Made you steal hither in the mornings—

Seb.   When
I used to look up 'neath the shrub-house here,
Till the red fire on its glazed windows spread
To a yellow haze?

Otti.   Ah—my sign was, the sun
Inflamed the sere side of yon chestnut-tree
Nipped by the first frost.

Seb.   You would always laugh
At my wet boots: I had to stride through grass
Over my ankles.

Otti   Then our crowning night!

Seb.   The July night?

Otti.   The day of it too, Sebald!
When heaven's pillars seemed o'erbowed with heat,
Its black-blue canopy suffered descend
Close on us both, to weigh down each to each,
And smother up all life except our life.
So lay we till the storm came.

Seb.   How it came!

Otti.   Buried in woods we lay, you recollect;
Swift ran the searching tempest overhead;
And ever and anon some bright white shaft
Burned through the pine-tree roof, here burned and
          there,
As if God's messenger through the close wood screen

Plunged and replunged his weapon at a venture,
Feeling for guilty thee and me: then broke
The thunder like a whole sea overhead—

    Seb.   Yes!

    Otti.—While I stretched myself upon you hands
To hands, my mouth to your hot mouth, and shook
All my locks loose, and covered you with them—
You, Sebald, the same you!

    Seb.   Slower, Ottima!

    Otti.   And as we lay—

    Seb.   Less vehemently! Love me!
Forgive me! Take not words, mere words, to heart!
Your breath is worse than wine. Breathe slow, speak
      slow!

Do not lean on me!

    Otti.   Sebald, as we lay,
Rising and falling only with our pants,
Who said, "Let death come now! 'T is right to die!
Right to be punished! Naught completes such bliss
But woe!" Who said that?

    Seb.   How did we ever rise?
Was 't that we slept? Why did it end?

    Otti.   I felt you
Taper into a point the ruffled ends
Of my loose locks 'twixt both your humid lips.
My hair is fallen now: knot it again!

    Seb.   I kiss you now, dear Ottima, now and now!

This way? Will you forgive me—be once more
My great queen?

    Otti.   Bind it thrice about my brow;
Crown me your queen, your spirit's arbitress,
Magnificent in sin. Say that!

    Seb.   I crown you
My great white queen, my spirit's arbitress,
Magnificent . . .

    [*From without is heard the voice of* PIPPA *singing*—

> The year's at the spring
> And day 's at the morn;
> Morning 's at seven;
> The hillside 's dew-pearled;
> The lark 's on the wing;
> The snail 's on the thorn:
> God 's in his heaven—
> All 's right with the world!

                           [PIPPA *passes.*

    Seb. God 's in his heaven! Do you hear that?
        Who spoke?
You, you spoke!

    Otti.   Oh—that little ragged girl!
She must have rested on the step: we give them
But this one holiday the whole year round.
Did you ever see our silk-mills—their inside?

There are ten silk-mills now belong to you.
She stoops to pick my double heartsease . . . Sh!
She does not hear: call you out louder!

   Seb.   Leave me!
Go, get your clothes on—dress those shoulders!

   Otti.   Sebald?

   Seb.   Wipe off that paint!   I hate you.

   Otti.   Miserable!

   Seb.   My God, and she is emptied of it now!
Outright now!—how miraculously gone
All of the grace—had she not strange grace once?
Why, the blank cheek hangs listless as it likes,
No purpose holds the features up together,
Only the cloven brow and puckered chin
Stay in their places: and the very hair,
That seemed to have a sort of life in it,
Drops, a dead web!

   Otti.   Speak to me—not of me!

   Seb.—That round great full-orbed face, where not
     an angle
Broke the delicious indolence—all broken!

   Otti.   To me—not of me!   Ungrateful, perjured
     cheat!
A coward too: but ingrate 's worse than all!
Beggar—my slave—a fawning, cringing lie!
Leave me! Betray me! I can see your drift!
A lie that walks and eats and drinks!

Seb.   My God!
'Those morbid olive faultless shoulder-blades—
I should have known there was no blood beneath!
   Otti. You hate me then? You hate me then?
   Seb.   To think
She would succeed in her absurd attempt,
And fascinate by sinning, show herself
Superior—guilt from its excess superior
To innocence! That little peasant's voice
Has righted all again. Though I be lost,
I know which is the better, never fear,
Of vice or virtue, purity or lust,
Nature or trick! I see what I have done,
Entirely now! Oh I am proud to feel
Such torments—let the world take credit thence—
I, having done my deed, pay too its price!
I hate, hate—curse you! God 's in his heaven!
   Otti.   —Me!
Me! no, no, Sebald, not yourself—kill me!
Mine is the whole crime. Do but kill me—then
Yourself—then—presently—first hear me speak!
I always meant to kill myself—wait, you!
Lean on my breast—not as a breast; don't love me
The more because you lean on me, my own
Heart's Sebald! There, there, both deaths presently!
   Seb. My brain is drowned now—quite drowned: all
      I feel

Is . . . is, at swift-recurring intervals,
A hurry-down within me, as of waters
Loosened to smother up some ghastly pit:
There they go—whirls from a black fiery sea!
   Otti.   Not me—to him, O God, be merciful!

Talk by the way, while PIPPA *is passing from the hill-*
   side to Orcana.   Foreign students of painting and
   sculpture, from Venice, assembled opposite the house
   of JULES, *a young French statuary, at Possagno.*

1st Student.   Attention! My own post is beneath
this window, but the pomegranate clump yonder will
hide three or four of you with a little squeezing, and
Schramm and his pipe must lie flat in the balcony.
Four, five—who 's a defaulter? We want everybody,
for Jules must not be suffered to hurt his bride when
the jest 's found out.

2d Stud.   All here! Only our poet 's away—never
having much meant to be present, moonstrike him!
The airs of that fellow, that Giovacchino! He was in
violent love with himself, and had a fair prospect of
thriving in his suit, so unmolested was it,—when suddenly a woman falls in love with him, too; and out of
pure jealousy he takes himself off to Trieste, immortal
poem and all: whereto is this prophetical epitaph
appended already, as Bluphocks assures me,—"*Here a
mammoth-poem lies, Fouled to death by butterflies.*"

His own fault, the simpleton! Instead of cramp coup-
lets, each like a knife in your entrails, he should write,
says Bluphocks, both classically and intelligibly.—
*Æsculapius, an Epic. Catalogue of the drugs: Hebe's
plaister—One strip Cools your lip. Phœbus' emulsion
—One bottle Clears your throttle. Mercury's bolus—
One box Cures* . . .

3d Stud. Subside, my fine fellow! If the marriage
was over by ten o'clock, Jules will certainly be here
in a minute with his bride.

2d Stud. Good!—only, so should the poet's muse
have been universally acceptable, says Bluphocks, *et
canibus nostris* . . . and Delia not better known to
our literary dogs than the boy Giovacchino!

1st Stud. To the point, now. Where 's Gottlieb,
the new-comer? Oh,—listen, Gottlieb, to what has
called down this piece of friendly vengeance on Jules,
of which we now assemble to witness the winding-up.
We are all agreed, all in a tale, observe, when Jules
shall burst out on us in a fury by and by: I am
spokesman—the verses that are to undeceive Jules
bear my name of Lutwyche—but each professes himself alike insulted by this strutting stone-squarer, who
came along from Paris to Munich, and thence with a
crowd of us to Venice and Possagno here, but proceeds
in a day or two alone again—oh, alone indubitably!—
to Rome and Florence. He, forsooth, take up his por-

tion with these dissolute, brutalized, heartless bun-
glers!—so he was heard to call us all. Now, is
Schramm brutalized, I should like to know? Am I
heartless?

Gottlieb. Why, somewhat heartless; for, suppose
Jules a coxcomb as much as you choose, still, for this
mere coxcombry, you will have brushed off—what do
folks style it?—the bloom of his life. Is it too late
to alter? These love letters now, you call his—I can't
laugh at them.

4th Stud. Because you never read the sham letters
of our inditing which drew forth these.

Gott. His discovery of the truth will be frightful.

4th Stud. That 's the joke. But you should have
joined us at the beginning: there 's no doubt he loves
the girl—loves a model he might hire by the hour!

Gott. See here! "He has been accustomed," he
writes, "to have Canova's women about him, in stone,
and the world's women beside him, in flesh; these
being as much below, as those above, his soul's aspira-
tion: but now he is to have the reality." There you
laugh again! I say, you wipe off the very dew of his
youth.

1st Stud. Schramm! (Take the pipe out of his
mouth, somebody!) Will Jules lose the bloom of his
youth?

Schramm. Nothing worth keeping is ever lost in

this world: look at a blossom—it drops presently, having done its service and lasted its time; but fruits succeed, and where would be the blossom's place could it continue? As well affirm that your eye is no longer in your body, because its earliest favorite, whatever it may have first loved to look on, is dead and done with—as that any affection is lost to the soul when its first object, whatever happened first to satisfy it, is superseded in due course. Keep but ever looking, whether with the body's eye or the mind's, and you will soon find something to look on! Has a man done wondering at women?—there follow men, dead and alive, to wonder at. Has he done wondering at men? —there's God to wonder at: and the faculty of wonder may be, at the same time, old and tired enough with respect to its first object, and yet young and fresh sufficiently, so far as concerns its novel one. Thus . . .

1st Stud. Put Schramm's pipe into his mouth again! There, you see! Well, this Jules . . . a wretched fribble—oh, I watched his disportings at Possagno, the other day! Canova's gallery—you know: there he marches first resolvedly past great works by the dozen without vouchsafing an eye: all at once he stops full at the *Psiche-fanciulla*—cannot pass that old acquaintance without a nod of encouragement— "In your new place, beauty? Then behave yourself as well here as at Munich—I see you!" Next he posts himself deliberately before the unfinished *Pietà* for half an hour without moving, till up he starts of a sudden, and thrusts his very nose into—I say, into— the group; by which gesture you are informed that precisely the sole point he had not fully mastered in Canova's practice was a certain method of using the drill in the articulation of the knee-joint—and that, likewise, has he mastered at length! Good-by therefore, to poor Canova—whose gallery no longer needs detain his successor Jules, the predestinated novel thinker in marble!

5th Stud. Tell him about the women: go on to the women!

1st Stud. Why, on that matter he could never be supercilious enough. How should we be other (he said) than the poor devils you see, with those debasing habits we cherish? He was not to wallow in that mire, at least: he would wait, and love only at the proper time, and meanwhile put up with the *Psiche-fanciulla.* Now, I happened to hear of a young Greek—real Greek girl at Malamocco; a true Islander, do you see, with Alciphron's "hair like sea-moss"—Schramm knows!—white and quiet as an apparition, and four- teen years old at farthest,—a daughter of Natalia, so she swears—that hag Natalia, who helps us to models at three *lire* an hour. We selected this girl for the heroine of our jest. So first, Jules received a scented letter—somebody had seen his Tydeus at the Academy, and my picture was nothing to it: a profound admirer bade him persevere—would make herself known to him ere long. (Paolina, my little friend of the *Fenice*, transcribes divinely.) And in due time, the mysterious correspondent gave certain hints of her peculiar charms—the pale cheeks, the black hair—whatever, in short, had struck us in our Malamocco model: we retained her name, too—Phene, which is, by interpretation, sea-eagle. Now, think of Jules finding himself distinguished from the herd of us by such a creature! In his very first answer he proposed marrying his monitress: and fancy us over these letters, two, three times a day, to receive and dispatch! I concocted the main of it: relations were in the way—secrecy must be observed—in fine, would he wed her on trust, and only speak to her when they were indissolubly united? St—st—Here they come!

6th Stud. Both of them! Heaven's love, speak softly, speak within yourselves!

5th Stud. Look at the bridegroom! Half his hair in storm and half in calm,—patted down over the left temple,—like a frothy cup one blows on to cool it: and the same old blouse that he murders the marble in.

2d Stud. Not a rich vest like yours, Hannibal Scratchy!—rich, that your face may the better set it off.

6th Stud. And the bride! Yes, sure enough, our Phene! Should you have known her in her clothes? How magnificently pale!

Gott. She does not also take it for earnest, I hope?

1st Stud. Oh, Natalia's concern, that is! We settle with Natalia.

6th Stud. She does not speak—has evidently let out no word. The only thing is, will she equally remember the rest of her lesson, and repeat correctly all those verses which are to break the secret to Jules?

Gott. How he gazes on her! Pity—pity!

1st Stud. They go in: now, silence! You three,—not nearer the window, mind, than that pomegranate: just where the little girl, who a few minutes ago passed us singing, is seated!

II. NOON

Over Orcana. The house of JULES, *who crosses its threshold with* PHENE: *she is silent, on which* JULES *begins—*

Do not die, Phene! I am yours now, you
Are mine now; let fate reach me how she likes,
If you 'll not die: so, never die! Sit here—
My work-room's single seat. I over-lean
This length of hair and lustrous front; they turn
Like an entire flower upward: eyes, lips, last

Your chin—no, last your throat turns: 't is their scent
Pulls down my face upon you. Nay, look ever
This one way till I change, grow you—I could
Change into you, beloved!

           You by me,
And I by you; this is your hand in mine,
And side by side we sit: all 's true. Thank God!
I have spoken: speak you!

                  O my life to come!
My Tydeus must be carved that 's there in clay;
Yet how be carved, with you about the room?
Where must I place you? When I think that once
This room-full of rough block-work seemed my heaven
Without you! Shall I ever work again,
Get fairly into my old ways again,
Bid each conception stand while, trait by trait,
My hand transfers its lineaments to stone?
Will my mere fancies live near you, their truth—
The live truth, passing and repassing me,
Sitting beside me?

           Now speak!

               Only first,
See, all your letters! Was 't not well contrived?
Their hiding-place is Psyche's robe; she keeps
Your letters next her skin: which drops out foremost?
Ah,—this that swam down like a first moonbeam
Into my world!

Again those eyes complete
Their melancholy survey, sweet and slow,
Of all my room holds; to return and rest
On me, with pity, yet some wonder too:
As if God bade some spirit plague a world,
And this were the one moment of surprise
And sorrow while she took her station, pausing
O'er what she sees, finds good, and must destroy!
What gaze you at? Those? Books, I told you of;
Let your first word to me rejoice them, too:
This minion, a Coluthus, writ in red,
Bistre and azure by Bessarion's scribe—
Read this line . . . no, shame—Homer's be the Greek
First breathed me from the lips of my Greek girl!
This Odyssey in coarse black vivid type
With faded yellow blossoms 'twixt page and page,
To mark great places with due gratitude;
"He said, and on Antinous directed
A bitter shaft" . . . a flower blots out the rest!
Again upon your search? My statues, then!
—Ah, do not mind that—better that will look
When cast in bronze—an Almaign Kaiser, that,
Swart-green and gold, with truncheon based on hip.
This, rather, turn to! What, unrecognized?
I thought you would have seen that here you sit
As I imagined you,—Hippolyta,
Naked upon her bright Numidian horse.

Recall you this then? "Carve in bold relief"—
So you commanded—"carve, against I come,
A Greek, in Athens, as our fashion was,
Feasting, bay-filleted and thunder-free,
Who rises 'neath the lifted myrtle-branch.
'Praise those who slew Hipparchas!' cry the guests,
'While o'er thy head the singer's myrtle waves
As erst above our champion: stand up, all!' "
See, I have labored to express your thought.
Quite round, a cluster of mere hands and arms
(Thrust in all senses, all ways, from all sides,
Only consenting at the branch's end
They strain toward) serves for frame to a sole face,
The Praiser's, in the centre: who with eyes
Sightless, so bend they back to light inside
His brain where visionary forms throng up,
Sings, minding not that palpitating arch
Of hands and arms, nor the quick drip of wine
From the drenched leaves o'erhead, nor crowns cast
        off,
Violet and parsley crowns to trample on—
Sings, pausing as the patron-ghosts approve,
Devoutly their unconquerable hymn.
But you must say a "well" to that—say "well!"
Because you gaze—am I fantastic, sweet?
Gaze like my very life's-stuff, marble—marbly
Even to the silence! Why, before I found

'The real flesh Phene, I inured myself
To see, throughout all nature, varied stuff
For better nature's birth by means of art:
With me, each substance tended to one form
Of beauty—to the human archetype.
On every side occurred suggestive germs
Of that—the tree, the flower—or take the fruit,—
Some rosy shape, continuing the peach,
Curved beewise o'er its bough; as rosy limbs,
Depending, nestled in the leaves; and just
From a cleft rose-peach the whole Dryad sprang.
But of the stuffs one can be master of,
How I divined their capabilities!
From the soft-rinded smoothening facile chalk
That yields your outline to the air's embrace,
Half-softened by a halo's pearly gloom;
Down to the crisp imperious steel, so sure
To cut its one confided thought clean out
Of all the world.   But marble!—'neath my tools
More pliable than jelly—as it were
Some clear primordial creature dug from depths
In the earth's heart, where itself breeds itself,
And whence all baser substance may be worked;
Refine it off to air, you may,—condense it
Down to the diamond;—is not metal there,
When o'er the sudden speck my chisel trips?
—Not flesh, as flake off flake I scale, approach,

Lay bare those bluish veins of blood asleep?
Lurks flame in no strange windings where, surprised
By the swift implement sent home at once,
Flushes and glowings radiate and hover
About its track?

     Phene? what—why is this?
That whitening cheek, those still dilating eyes!
Ah, you will die—I knew that you would die!

 PHENE *begins, on his having long remained silent.*

Now the end 's coming; to be sure, it must
Have ended sometime! Tush, why need I speak
Their foolish speech? I cannot bring to mind
One half of it, beside: and do not care
For old Natalia now, nor any of them.
Oh, you—what are you?—if I do not try
To say the words Natalia made me learn,
To please your friends,—it is to keep myself
Where your voice lifted me, by letting that
Proceed: but can it? Even you, perhaps,
Cannot take up, now you have once let fall,
The music's life, and me along with that—
No, or you would! We 'll stay, then, as we are:
Above the world.

     You creature with the eyes!
If I could look forever up to them,
As now you let me,—I believe, all sin,

All memory of wrong done, suffering borne,
Would drop down, low and lower, to the earth
Whence all that 's low comes, and there touch and
        stay
—Never to overtake the rest of me,
All that, unspotted, reaches up to you,
Drawn by those eyes! What rises is myself,
Not me the shame and suffering; but they sink,
Are left, I rise above them. Keep me so,
Above the world!

                        But you sink, for your eyes
Are altering—altered! Stay—"I love you, love" . . .
I could prevent it if I understood:
More of your words to me: was 't in the tone
Or the words, your power?

                        Or stay—I will repeat
Their speech, if that contents you! Only change
No more, and I shall find it presently
Far back here, in the brain yourself filled up.
Natalia threatened me that harm should follow
Unless I spoke their lesson to the end,
But harm to me, I thought she meant, not you.
Your friends,—Natalia said they were your friends
And meant you well,—because, I doubted it.
Observing (what was very strange to see)
On every face, so different in all else.

The same smile girls like me are used to bear,
But never men, men cannot stoop so low;
Yet your friends, speaking of you, used that smile.
That hateful smirk of boundless self-conceit
Which seems to take possession of the world
And make of God a tame confederate,
Purveyor to their appetites . . . you know!
But still Natalia said they were your friends,
And they assented though they smiled the more,
And all came round me,—that thin Englishman
With light lank hair seemed leader of the rest;
He held a paper—"What we want," said he,
Ending some explanation to his friends—
"Is something slow, involved and mystical,
To hold Jules long in doubt, yet take his taste
And lure him on until, at innermost
Where he seeks sweetness' soul, he may find—this!
—As in the apple's core, the noisome fly:
For insects on the rind are seen at once,
And brushed aside as soon, but this is found
Only when on the lips or loathing tongue."
And so he read what I have got by heart:
I 'll speak it,—"Do not die, love! I am yours" . . .
No—is not that, or like that, part of words
Yourself began by speaking? Strange to lose
What cost such pains to learn! Is this more right?

I am a painter who cannot paint;
In my life, a devil rather than saint;
In my brain, as poor a creature too:
No end to all I cannot do!
Yet do one thing at least I can—
Love a man or hate a man
Supremely: thus my lore began.
Through the Valley of Love I went,
In the lovingest spot to abide,
And just on the verge where I pitched my tent,
I found Hate dwelling beside.
(Let the Bridegroom ask what the painter meant,
Of his Bride, of the peerless Bride!)
And further, I traversed Hate's grove,
In the hatefullest nook to dwell;
But lo, where I flung myself prone, couched Love
Where the shadow threefold fell.
(The meaning—those black bride's-eyes above,
Not a painter's lip should tell!)

"And here," said he, "Jules probably will ask,
'You have black eyes, Love,—you are, sure enough,
My peerless bride,—then do you tell indeed
What needs some explanation! What means this?'"
—And I am to go on, without a word—

So, I grew wise in Love and Hate,
From simple that I was of late.

Once, when I loved, I would enlace
Breast, eyelids, hands, feet, form and face
Of her I loved, in one embrace—
As if by mere love I could love immensely!
Once, when I hated, I would plunge
My sword, and wipe with the first lunge
My foe's whole life out like a sponge—
As if by mere hate I could hate intensely!
But now I am wiser, know better the fashion
How passion seeks aid from its opposite passion:
And if I see cause to love more, hate more
Than ever man loved, ever hated before—
And seek in the Valley of Love
The nest, or the nook in Hate's Grove
Where my soul may surely reach
The essence, naught less, of each,
The Hate of all Hates, the Love
Of all Loves, in the Valley or Grove,—
I find them the very warders
Each of the other's borders.
When I love most, Love is disguised
In Hate; and when Hate is surprised
In Love, then I hate most: ask
How Love smiles through Hate's iron casque,
Hate grins through Love's rose-braided mask,—
And how, having hated thee,
I sought long and painfully

To reach thy heart, nor prick
The skin but pierce to the quick—
Ask this, my Jules, and be answered straight
By thy bride—how the painter Lutwyche can hate!

JULES *interposes.*

Lutwyche! Who else? But all of them, no doubt,
Hated me: they at Venice—presently
Their turn, however! You I shall not meet:
If I dreamed, saying this would wake me.

Keep

What 's here, the gold—we cannot meet again,
Consider! and the money was but meant
For two years' travel, which is over now,
All chance or hope or care or need of it.
This—and what comes from selling these, my casts
And books and medals, except . . . let them go
Together, so the produce keeps you safe
Out of Natalia's clutches! If by chance
(For all 's chance here) I should survive the gang
At Venice, root out all fifteen of them,
We might meet somewhere, since the world is wide.
    [*From without is heard the voice of* PIPPA, *singing—*

Give her but a least excuse to love me!
When—where—
How—can this arm establish her above me,

If fortune fixed her as my lady there,
There already, to eternally reprove me?
("Hist!"—said Kate the Queen;
But "Oh!" cried the maiden, binding her tresses,
" 'Tis only a page that carols unseen,
Crumbling your hounds their messes!")

Is she wronged?—To the rescue of her honor,
My heart!
Is she poor?—What costs it to be styled a donor?
Merely an earth to cleave, a sea to part.
But that fortune should have thrust all this upon
    her!
("Nay, list!"—bade Kate the Queen;
And still cried the maiden, binding her tresses,
" 'T is only a page that carols unseen,
Fitting your hawks their jesses!")

                                [PIPPA *passes*

JULES *resumes.*

What name was that the little girl sang forth?
Kate? The Cornaro, doubtless, who renounced
The crown of Cyprus to be lady here
At Asolo, where still her memory stays,
And peasants sing how once a certain page
Pined for the grace of her so far above
His power of doing good to, "Kate the Queen—

She never could be wronged, be poor," he sighed,
"Need him to help her!"

                          Yes, a bitter thing
To see our lady above all need of us;
Yet so we look ere we will love; not I,
But the world looks so. If whoever loves
Must be, in some sort, god or worshipper,
The blessing or the blest one, queen or page,
Why should we always choose the page's part?
Here is a woman with utter need of me,—
I find myself queen here, it seems!

                          How strange!
Look at the woman here with the new soul,
Like my own Psyche,—fresh upon her lips
Alit, the visionary butterfly,
Waiting my word to enter and make bright,
Or flutter off and leave all blank as first.
This body had no soul before, but slept
Or stirred, was beauteous or ungainly, free
From taint or foul with stain, as outward things
Fastened their image on its passiveness:
Now, it will wake, feel, live—or die again!
Shall to produce form out of unshaped stuff
Be Art—and further, to evoke a soul
From form be nothing? This new soul is mine!

Now, to kill Lutwyche, what would that do?—save
A wretched dauber, men will hoot to death
Without me, from their hooting. Oh, to hear
God's voice plain as I heard it first, before
They broke in with their laughter! I heard them
Henceforth, not God.

                  To Ancona—Greece—some isle!
I wanted silence only; there is clay
Everywhere. One may do whate'er one likes
In Art: the only thing is, to make sure
That one does like it—which takes pains to know.
  Scatter all this, my Phene—this mad dream!
Who, what is Lutwyche, what Natalia's friends,
What the whole world except our love—my own,
Own Phene? But I told you, did I not,
Ere night we travel for your land—some isle
With the sea's silence on it? Stand aside—
I do but break these paltry models up
To begin Art afresh. Meet Lutwyche, I—
And save him from my statue meeting him?
Some unsuspected isle in the far seas!
Like a god going through his world, there stands
One mountain for a moment in the dusk,
Whole brotherhoods of cedars on its brow:
And you are ever by me while I gaze

—Are in my arms as now—as now—as now!
Some unsuspected isle in the far seas!
Some unsuspected isle in far-off seas!

Talk by the way, while Pippa *is passing from Orcana
to the Turret. Two or three of the Austrian Police
loitering with* Bluphocks, *an English vagabond,
just in view of the Turret.*

Bluphocks.[1] So, that is your Pippa, the little girl
who passed us singing? Well, your Bishop's Intendant's money shall be honestly earned:—now, don't
make me that sour face because I bring the Bishop's
name into the business; we know he can have nothing
to do with such horrors: we know that he is a saint
and all that a bishop should be, who is a great man
beside. *Oh were but every worm a maggot, Every
fly a grip, Every bough a Christmas fagot, Every
tune a jig!* In fact, I have abjured all religions; but
the last I inclined to was the Armenian: for I have
travelled, do you see, and at Koenigsberg, Prussia
Improper (so styled because there 's a sort of bleak
hungry sun there), you might remark, over a vener-
able house-porch, a certain Chaldee inscription; and
brief as it is, a mere glance at it used absolutely to
change the mood of every bearded passenger. In

[1] "He maketh his sun to rise on the evil and on the good,
and sendeth rain on the just and on the unjust."

they turned, one and all; the young and lightsome, with no irreverent pause, the aged and decrepit, with a sensible alacrity: 't was the Grand Rabbi's abode, in short.   Struck with curiosity, I lost no time in learning Syriac—(these are vowels, you dogs,—follow my stick's end in the mud—*Celarent, Darii, Ferio!*) and one morning presented myself, spelling-book in hand, a, b, c,—I picked it out letter by letter, and what was the purport of this miraculous posy? Some cherished legend of the past, you 'll say—*"How Moses hocus-pocussed Egypt's land with fly and locust,"*— or, *"How to Jonah sounded harshish, Get thee up and go to Tarshish,"*—or *"How the angel meeting Balaam, Straight his ass returned a salaam."*   In no wise! *"Shackabrack—Boach—somebody or other—Isaach, Re-cei-ver, Pur-cha-ser and Ex-chan-ger of—Stolen Goods!"*   So, talk to me of the religion of a bishop! I have renounced all bishops save Bishop Beveridge! —mean to live so—and die—*As some Greek dog-sage, dead and merry, Hellward bound in Charon's wherry. With food for both worlds, under and upper.   Lupine-seed and Hecate's supper, And never an obolus . . .* (though thanks to you, or this Intendant through you, or this Bishop through his Intendant—I possess a burning pocket-full of *zwanzigers*) . . .*To pay the Stygian Ferry!*

1st Policeman.   There is the girl, then; go and deserve them the moment you have pointed out to us Signor Luigi and his mother. [*To the rest.*] I have been noticing a house yonder, this long while: not a shutter unclosed since morning!

2d Pol. Old Luca Gaddi's, that owns the silk-mills here: he dozes by the hour, wakes up, sighs deeply, says he should like to be Prince Metternich, and then dozes again, after having bidden young Sebald, the foreigner, set his wife to playing draughts. Never molest such a household, they mean well.

Blup. Only, cannot you tell me something of this little Pippa, I must have to do with? One could make something of that name. Pippa—that is, short for Felippa—rhyming to *Panurge consults Hertrippa—Believest thou, King Agrippa?* Something might be done with that name.

2d Pol. Put into rhyme that your head and a ripe muskmelon would not be dear at half a *zwanziger!* Leave this fooling, and look out; the afternoon 's over or nearly so.

3d Pol. Where in this passport of Signor Luigi does our Principal instruct you to watch him so narrowly? There? What 's there beside a simple signature? (That English fool 's busy watching.)

2d Pol. Flourish all round—"Put all possible obstacles in his way;" oblong dot at the end—"Detain him till further advices reach you;" scratch at bot-

tom—"Send him back on pretence of some informality
in the above;" ink-spirt on righthand side (which is
the case here)—"Arrest him at once." Why and
wherefore, I don't concern myself, but my instructions
amount to this: if Signor Luigi leaves home to-night
for Vienna—well and good, the passport deposed with
us for our *visa* is really for his own use, they have
misinformed the Office, and he means well; but let
him stay over to-night—there has been the pretence
we suspect, the accounts of his corresponding and
holding intelligence with the Carbonari are correct,
we arrest him at once, to-morrow comes Venice, and
presently Spielberg. Bluphocks makes the signal,
sure enough! That is he, entering the turret with his
mother, no doubt.

III. EVENING

Inside the Turret on the Hill above Asolo. LUIGI *and*
his MOTHER *entering.*

   Mother. If there blew wind, you 'd hear a long
         sigh, easing
The utmost heaviness of music's heart.
   Luigi. Here in the archway?
   Mother.   Oh no, no—in farther,
Where the echo is made, on the ridge.

Luigi.   Here surely, then.
How plain the tap of my heel as I leaped up!
Hark—"Lucius Junius!" The very ghost of a voice
Whose body is caught and kept by . . . what are
        those?
Mere withered wallflowers, waving overhead?
They seem an elvish group with thin bleached hair
That lean out of their topmost fortress—look
And listen, mountain men, to what we say,
Hand under chin of each grave earthy face.
Up and show faces all of you!—"All of you!"
That 's the king dwarf with the scarlet comb; old
        Franz,
Come down and meet your fate? Hark—"Meet your
        fate!"
Mother. Let him not meet it, my Luigi—do not
Go to his City! Putting crime aside,
Half of these ills of Italy are feigned:
Your Pellicos and writers for effect,
Write for effect.
Luigi.   Hush! Say A writes, and B.
Mother. These A's and B's write for effect, I say.
Then, evil is in its nature loud, while good
Is silent; you hear each petty injury,
None of his virtues; he is old beside,
Quiet and kind, and densely stupid. Why
Do A and B kill not him themselves?

Luigi.   They teach

Others to kill him—me—and, if I fail,

Others to succeed; now, if A tried and failed,

I could not teach that: mine 's the lesser task.

Mother, they visit night by night . . .

   Mother.   —You, Luigi?

Ah, will you let me tell you what you are?

   Luigi.   Why not?   Oh, the one thing you fear to
      hint,

You may assure yourself I say and say

Ever to myself.   At times—nay, even as now

We sit—I think my mind is touched, suspect

All is not sound: but is not knowing that,

What constitutes one sane or otherwise?

I know I am thus—so, all is right again.

I laugh at myself as through the town I walk,

And see men merry as if no Italy

Were suffering; then I ponder—"I am rich,

Young, healthy; why should this fact trouble me,

More than it troubles these?"   But it does trouble

No, trouble 's a bad word: for as I walk

There 's springing and melody and giddiness,

And old quaint turns and passages of my youth,

Dreams long forgotten, little in themselves,

Return to me—whatever may amuse me:

And earth seems in a truce with me, and heaven

Accords with me, all things suspend their strife,

The very cicala laughs "There goes he, and there!
Feast him, the time is short; he is on his way
For the world's sake: feast him this once, our friend!"
And in return for all this, I can trip
Cheerfully up the scaffold-steps. I go
This evening, mother!
    Mother.   But mistrust yourself—
Mistrust the judgment you pronounce on him!
    Luigi. Oh, there I feel—am sure that I am right!
    Mother. Mistrust your judgment then, of the mere
        means
To this wild enterprise: say, you are right,—
How should one in your state e'er bring to pass
What would require a cool head, a cool heart,
And a calm hand? You never will escape.
    Luigi. Escape? To even wish that, would spoil all.
The dying is best part of it. Too much
Have I enjoyed these fifteen years of mine,
To leave myself excuse for longer life:
Was not life pressed down, running o'er with joy,
That I might finish with it ere my fellows
Who, sparelier feasted, make a longer stay?
I was put at the board-head, helped to all
At first; I rise up happy and content.
God must be glad one loves his world so much.
I can give news of earth to all the dead
Who ask me:—last year's sunsets, and great stars

Which had a right to come first and see ebb
The crimson wave that drifts the sun away—
Those crescent moons with notched and burning rim,
That strengthened into sharp fire, and there stood,
Impatient of the azure—and that day
In March, a double rainbow stopped the storm—
May's warm slow yellow moonlit summer nights—
Gone are they, but I have them in my soul!

   Mother. (He will not go!)

   Luigi.   You smile at me? 'T is true,—
Voluptuousness, grotesqueness, ghastliness,
Environ my devotedness as quaintly
As round about some antique altar wreathe
The rose festoons, goats' horns, and oxen's skulls.

   Mother. See now: you reach the city, you must
      cross
His threshold—how?

   Luigi.   Oh, that's if we conspired!
Then would come pains in plenty, as you guess—
But guess not how the qualities most fit
For such an office, qualities I have,
Would little stead me, otherwise employed,
Yet prove of rarest merit only here.
Every one knows for what his excellence
Will serve, but no one ever will consider
For what his worst defect might serve: and yet
Have you not seen me range our coppice yonder

In search of a distorted ash?—I find
The wry spoilt branch a natural perfect **bow.**
Fancy the thrice-sage, thrice-precautioned' **man**
Arriving at the palace on my errand!
No, no! I have a handsome dress packed up—
White satin here, to set off my black hair;
In I shall march—for you may watch your life out
Behind thick walls, make friends there to betray **you;**
More than one man spoils everything. **March
        straight—**
Only, no clumsy knife to fumble for,
Take the great gate, and walk (not saunter) on
Through guards and guards— I have rehearsed **it all**
Inside the turret here a hundred times.
Don't ask the way of whom you meet, observe!
But where they cluster thickliest is the door
Of doors; they 'll let you pass—they 'll never blab
Each to the other, he knows not the favorite,
Whence he is bound and what 's his business now,
Walk in—straight up to him; you have no knife:
Be prompt, how should he scream? Then, out **with
        you!**
Italy, Italy, my Italy!
You 're free, you 're free! Oh mother, I could' **dream**
They got about me—Andrea from his exile,
Pier from his dungeon, Gualtier from his grave!

Mother.   Well, you shall go.   Yet seems this patri-
   otism
The easiest virtue for a selfish man
To acquire: he loves himself—and next, the world—
If he must love beyond,—but naught between:
As a short-sighted man sees naught midway
His body and the sun above.   But you
Are my adored Luigi, ever obedient
To my least wish, and running o'er with love:
I could not call you cruel or unkind.
Once more, your ground for killing him!—then go!
   Luigi.   Now do you try me, or make sport of me?
How first the Austrians got these provinces . . .
(If that is all, I 'll satisfy you soon)
—Never by conquest but by cunning, for
That treaty whereby . . .
      Mother.   Well?
      Luigi.   (Sure, he 's arrived,
The tell-tale cuckoo: spring 's his confidant,
And he lets out her April purposes!)
Or . . . better go at once to modern time.
He has . . . they have . . . in fact, I understand
But can't restate the matter; that 's my boast:
Others could reason it out to you, and prove
Things they have made me feel.
      Mother.   Why go to-night?

Morn 's for adventure. Jupiter is now
A morning-star. I cannot hear you, Luigi!
    Luigi. "I am the bright and morning-star," saith
        God—
And, "to such an one I give the morning-star."
The gift of the morning-star! Have I God's gift
Of the morning-star?
    Mother.   Chiara will love to see
That Jupiter an evening-star next June.
    Luigi. True, mother. Well for those who live
        through June!
Great noontides, thunder-storms, all glaring pomps
That triumph at the heels of June the god
Leading his revel through our leafy world.
Yes, Chiara will be here.
    Mother.   In June: remember,
Yourself appointed that month for her coming.
    Luigi. Was that low noise the echo?
    Mother.   The night-wind.
She must be grown—with her blue eyes upturned
As if life were one long and sweet surprise:
In June she comes.
    Luigi.   We were to see together
The Titian at Treviso. There, again!
    [*From without is heard the voice of* PIPPA, *singing—*

      A king lived long ago,
      In the morning of the world,

When earth was nigher heaven than now;
And the king's locks curled,
Disparting o'er a forehead full
As the milk-white space 'twixt horn and horn
Of some sacrificial bull—
Only calm as a babe new-born:
For he was got to a sleepy mood,
So safe from all decrepitude,
Age with its bane, so sure gone by,
(The gods so loved him while he dreamed)
That, having lived thus long, there seemed
No need the king should ever die.

Luigi. No need that sort of king should ever die!

Among the rocks his city was:
Before his palace, in the sun,
He sat to see his people pass,
And judge them every one
From its threshold of smooth stone.
They haled him many a valley-thief
Caught in the sheep-pens, robber-chief
Swarthy and shameless, beggar-cheat,
Spy-prowler, or rough pirate found
On the sea-sand left aground;
And sometimes clung about his feet,
With bleeding lip and burning cheek,
A woman, bitterest wrong to speak

Of one with sullen thickset brows:
And sometimes from the prison-house
The angry priests a pale wretch brought,
Who through some chink had pushed and pressed
On knees and elbows, belly and breast,
Worm-like into the temple,—caught
He was by the very god,
Who ever in the darkness strode
Backward and forward, keeping watch
O'er his brazen bowls, such rogues to catch!
These, all and every one,
The king judged, sitting in the sun.

Luigi.   That king should still judge sitting in the
        sun!

His councillors, on left and right,
Looked anxious up,—but no surprise
Disturbed the king's old smiling eyes
Where the very blue had turned to white.
'T is said, a Python scared one day
The breathless city, till he came,
With forky tongue and eyes on flame,
Where the old king sat to judge alway;
But when he saw the sweepy hair
Girt with a crown of berries rare
Which the god will hardly give to wear
*To the maiden who singeth, dancing bare_*

In the altar-smoke by the pine-torch lights,
At his wondrous forest rites,—
Seeing this, he did not dare
Approach that threshold in the sun,
Assault the old king smiling there.
Such grace had kings when the world begun!

[PIPPA *passes.*

Luigi.   And such grace have they, now that the
world ends!
The Python at the city, on the throne,
And brave men, God would crown for slaying him,
Lurk in by-corners lest they fall his prey.
Are crowns yet to be won in this late time,
Which weakness makes me hesitate to reach?
'T is God's voice calls: how could I stay?   Farewell!

Talk by the way, while PIPPA *is passing from the Tur-*
ret to the Bishop's Brother's House, close to the
Duomo S. Maria.   Poor GIRLS *sitting on the steps.*

1st *Girl.*   There goes a swallow to Venice—the stout
seafarer!
Seeing those birds fly, makes one wish for wings.
Let us all wish; you, wish first!
2d *Girl.*   I?   This sunset
To finish.
3d *Girl.*   That old—somebody I know,
Graver and older than my grandfather,

To give me the same treat he gave last week—
Feeding me on his knee with fig-peckers,
Lampreys and red Breganze-wine, and mumbling
The while some folly about how well I fare,
Let sit and eat my supper quietly:
Since had he not himself been late this morning
Detained at—never mind where,—had he not . . .
"Eh, baggage, had I not!"—

    2d Girl.   How she can lie!

    3d Girl.   Look there—by the nails!

    2d Girl.   What makes your fingers red?

    3d Girl.   Dipping them into wine to write bad
        words with

On the bright table: how he laughed!

    1st Girl.   My turn.

Spring 's come and summer 's coming. I would wear
A long loose gown, down to the feet and hands,
With plaits here, close about the throat, all day;
And all night lie, the cool long nights, in bed;
And have new milk to drink, apples to eat,
Deuzans and junetings, leather-coats . . . ah, I should
    say,
This is away in the fields—miles!

    3d Girl.   Say at once
You 'd be at home: she 'd always be at home!
Now comes the story of the farm among
The cherry orchards, and how April snowed

White blossoms on her as she ran. Why, fool,
They 've rubbed the chalk-mark out, how tall you
     were,
Twisted your starling's neck, broken his cage,
Made a dung-hill of your garden!
    1st *Girl.*   They destroy
My garden since I left them? well—perhaps
I would have done so: so I hope they have!
A fig-tree curled out of our cottage wall;
They called it mine, I have forgotten why,
It must have been there long ere I was born:
Cric—cric—I think I hear the wasps o'erhead
Pricking the papers strung to flutter there
And keep off birds in fruit-time—coarse long papers,
And the wasps eat them, prick them through and
     through.
   3d *Girl.* How her mouth twitches! Where was I?
     —before
She broke in with her wishes and long gowns
And wasps—would I be such a fool!—Oh, here!
This is my way: I answer every one
Who asks me why I make so much of him—
(If you say, "you love him"—straight "he 'll not be
     gulled!")
"He that seduced me when I was a girl
Thus high—had eyes like yours, or hair like yours,
Brown, red, white,"—as the case may be: that pleases!

See how that beetle burnishes in the path!
There sparkles he along the dust: and, there—
Your journey to that maize-tuft spoiled at least!

  1st Girl.   When I was young, they said if you killed
    one
Of those sunshiny beetles, that his friend
Up there, would shine no more that day nor next.

  2d Girl. When you were young? Nor are you
    young, that 's true.
How your plump arms, that were, have dropped away!
Why, I can span them. Cecco beats you still?
No matter, so you keep your curious hair.
I wish they 'd find a way to dye our hair
Your color—any lighter tint, indeed,
Than black: the men say they are sick of black,
Black eyes, black hair!

  4th Girl.   Sick of yours, like enough
Do you pretend you ever tasted lampreys
And ortolans? Giovita, of the palace,
Engaged (but there 's no trusting him) to slice me
Polenta with a knife that had cut up
An ortolan.

  2d Girl. Why, there! Is not that Pippa
We are to talk to, under the window,—quick!—
Where the lights are?

  1st Girl. That she? No, or she would sing,
For the Intendant said . . .

3d *Girl*.   Oh, you sing first!
Then, if she listens and comes close . . . I 'll tell you,—
Sing that song the young English noble made,
Who took you for the purest of the pure,
And' meant to leave the world for you—what fun!
    2d *Girl*. [*Sings.*]

   You 'll love me yet!—and I can tarry
     Your love's protracted growing:
   June reared that bunch of flowers you carry,
     From seeds of April's sowing.

   I plant a heartfull now: some seed
     At least is sure to strike,
   And yield—what you 'll not pluck indeed,
     Not love, but, may be, like.

   You 'll look at least on love's remains,
     A grave's one violet:
   Your look?—that pays a thousand pains.
     What 's death? You 'll love me yet!

   3d *Girl*. [*To* PIPPA *who approaches.*] Oh, you
may come closer—we shall not eat you! Why, you
seem the very person that the great rich handsome
Englishman has fallen so violently in love with. I 'll
tell you all about it.

IV. NIGHT

Inside the Palace by the Duomo. MONSIGNOR, *dis-*
missing his Attendants.

Monsignor. Thanks, friends, many thanks! I
chiefly desire life now, that I may recompense every
one of you. Most I know something of already.
What, a repast prepared? *Benedicto benedicatur* . . .
ugh, ugh! Where was I? Oh, as you were remarking,
Ugo, the weather is mild, very unlike winter-weather:
but I am a Sicilian, you know, and shiver in your
Julys here. To be sure, when 't was full summer at
Messina, as we priests used to cross in procession the
great square on Assumption Day, you might see our
thickest yellow tapers twist suddenly in two, each
like a falling star, or sink down on themselves in a
gore of wax. But go, my friends, but go! [*To the*
Intendant.] Not you, Ugo! [*The others leave the*
apartment.] I have long wanted to converse with
you, Ugo.

Intendant. Uguccio—

Mon. . . . 'guccio Stefani, man! of Ascoli, Fermo
and Fossombruno;—what I do need instructing about,
are these accounts of your administration of my poor
brother's affairs. Ugh! I shall never get through a
third part of your accounts; take some of these dain-

ties before we attempt it, however. Are you bashful
to that degree? For me, a crust and water suffice.

Inten. Do you choose this especial night to question me?

Mon. This night, Ugo. You have managed my
late brother's affairs since the death of our elder
brother: fourteen years and a month, all but three
days. On the Third of December, I find him . . .

Inten. If you have so intimate an acquaintance
with your brother's affairs, you will be tender of turn-
ing so far back: they will hardly bear looking into.
so far back.

Mon. Ay, ay, ugh, ugh,—nothing but disappointments here below! I remark a considerable payment
made to yourself on this Third of December. Talk
of disappointments! There was a young fellow here,
Jules, a foreign sculptor I did my utmost to advance,
that the Church might be a gainer by us both: he was
going on hopefully enough, and of a sudden he notifies
to me some marvellous change that has happened in
his notions of Art. Here 's his letter,—"He never had
a clearly conceived Ideal within his brain till to-day.
Yet since his hand could manage a chisel, he has prac-
tised expressing other men's Ideals; and, in the very
perfection he has attained to, he foresees an ultimate
failure: his unconscious hand will pursue its pre-
scribed course of old years, and will reproduce with a

fatal expertness the ancient types, let the novel one
appear never so palpably to his spirit. There is but
one method of escape: confiding the virgin type to as
chaste a hand, he will turn painter instead of sculptor,
and paint, not carve, its characteristics,"—strike out,
I dare say, a school like Correggio: how think you,
Ugo?

Inten.   Is Correggio a painter?

Mon.   Foolish Jules! and yet, after all, why foolish? He may—probably will—fail egregiously; but
if there should arise a new painter, will it not be in
some such way, by a poet now, or a musician (spirits
who have conceived and perfected an Ideal through
some other channel), transferring it to this, and escap-
ing our conventional roads by pure ignorance of them;
eh, Ugo? If you have no appetite, talk at least, Ugo!

Inten.   Sir, I can submit no longer to this course
of yours. First, you select the group of which I
formed one,—next you thin it gradually,—always
retaining me with your smile,—and so do you proceed till you have fairly got me alone with you between four stone walls. And now then? Let this
farce, this chatter end now: what is it you want with
me?

Mon.   Ugo!

Inten.   From the instant you arrived, I felt your
smile on me as you questioned me about this and the

other article in those papers—why your brother should
have given me this villa, that *podere*,—and your nod
at the end meant,—what?

Mon. Possibly that I wished for no loud talk here.
If once you set me coughing, Ugo!—

Inten. I have your brother's hand and seal to all
I possess: now ask me what for! what service I did
him—ask me!

Mon. I would better not: I should rip up old dis-
graces, let out my poor brother's weaknesses. By the
way, Maffeo of Forli, (which, I forgot to observe, is
your true name,) was the interdict ever taken off you
for robbing that church at Cesena?

Inten. No, nor needs be: for when I murdered your
brother's friend, Pasquale, for him . . .

Mon. Ah, he employed you in that business, did
he? Well, I must let you keep, as you say, this villa
and that *podere*, for fear the world should find out
my relations were of so indifferent a stamp? Maffeo,
my family is the oldest in Messina, and century after
century have my progenitors gone on polluting themselves with every wickedness under heaven: my own
father . . . rest his soul!—I have, I know, a chapel to
support that it may rest: my dear two dead brothers
were,—what you know tolerably well; I, the youngest,
might have rivalled them in vice, if not in wealth:
but from my boyhood I came out from among them,

and so am not partaker of their plagues. My glory
springs from another source; or if from this, by contrast only,—for I, the bishop, am the brother of your
employers, Ugo. I hope to repair some of their wrong,
however; so far as my brother's ill-gotten treasure
reverts to me, I can stop the consequences of his
crime: and not one *soldo* shall escape me. Maffeo,
the sword we quiet men spurn away, you shrewd
knaves pick up and commit murders with; what op-
portunities the virtuous forego, the villanous seize.
Because, to pleasure myself apart from other consid-
erations, my food would be millet-cake, my dress
sackcloth, and my couch straw,—am I therefore to
let you, the off-scouring of the earth, seduce the poor
and ignorant by appropriating a pomp these will be
sure to think lessens the abominations so unaccount-
ably and exclusively associated with it? Must I let
villas and *poderi* go to you, a murderer and thief,
that you may beget by means of them other mur-
derers and thieves? No—if my cough would but allow
me to speak!

Inten. What am I to expect? You are going to
punish me?

Mon. Must punish you, Maffeo. I cannot afford
to cast away a chance. I have whole centuries of sin
to redeem, and only a month or two of life to do it in.
How should I dare to say . . .

Inten. "Forgive us our trespasses"?

Mon. My friend, it is because I avow myself a very worm, sinful beyond measure, that I reject a line of conduct you would applaud perhaps. Shall I proceed, as it were, a-pardoning?—I?—who have no symptom of reason to assume that aught less than my strenuousest efforts will keep myself out of mortal sin, much less keep others out. No: I do trespass, but will not double that by allowing you to trespass.

Inten. And suppose the villas are not your brother's to give, nor yours to take? Oh, you are hasty enough just now!

Mon. 1, 2—Nº 3!—ay, can you read the substance of a letter, Nº 3, I have received from Rome? It is precisely on the ground there mentioned, of the suspicion I have that a certain child of my late elder brother, who would have succeeded to his estates, was murdered in infancy by you, Maffeo, at the instigation of my late younger brother—that the Pontiff enjoins on me not merely the bringing that Maffeo to condign punishment, but the taking all pains, as guardian of the infant's heritage for the Church, to recover it parcel by parcel, howsoever, whensoever, and wheresoever. While you are now gnawing those fingers, the police are engaged in sealing up your papers, Maffeo, and the mere raising my voice brings my people from the next room to dispose of yourself

But I want you to confess quietly, and save me raising my voice. Why, man, do I not know the old
story? The heir between the succeeding heir, and this
heir's ruffianly instrument, and their complot's effect,
and the life of fear and bribes and ominous smiling
silence? Did you throttle or stab my brother's infant?
Come now!

Inten. So old a story, and tell it no better? When
did such an instrument ever produce such an effect?
Either the child smiles in his face; or, most likely,
he is not fool enough to put himself in the employer's
power so thoroughly: the child is always ready to
produce—as you say—howsoever, wheresoever, and
whensoever.

Mon. Liar.

Inten. Strike me? Ah, so might a father chas-
tise! I shall sleep soundly to-night at least, though
the gallows await me to-morrow; for what a life did
I lead! Carlo of Cesena reminds me of his conniv-
ance, every time I pay his annuity; which happens
commonly thrice a year. If I remonstrate, he will
confess all to the good bishop—you!

Mon. I see through the trick, caitiff! I would you
spoke truth for once. All shall be sifted, however—
seven times sifted.

Inten. And how my absurd riches encumbered me!

I dared not lay claim to above half my possessions.
Let me but once unbosom myself, glorify Heaven,
and die!

Sir, you are no brutal dastardly idiot like your
brother I frightened to death: let us understand one
another. Sir, I will make away with her for you—
the girl—here close at hand; not the stupid obvious
kind of killing; do not speak—know nothing of her
nor of me! I see her every day—saw her this morning: of course there is to be no killing; but at Rome
the courtesans perish off every three years, and I can
entice her thither—have indeed begun operations
already. There 's a certain lusty blue-eyed florid-
complexioned English knave, I and the Police employ
occasionally. You assent, I perceive—no, that 's not
it—assent I do not say—but you will let me convert
my present havings and holdings into cash, and give
me time to cross the Alps? 'T is but a little black-
eyed pretty singing Felippa, gay silk-winding girl.
I have kept her out of harm's way up to this present;
for I always intended to make your life a plague to
you with her. 'T is as well settled once and forever.
Some women I have procured will pass Bluphocks,
my handsome scoundrel, off for somebody; and once
Pippa entangled!—you conceive? Through her singing? Is it a bargain?

[From without is heard the voice of PIPPA, *singing—*

Overhead the tree-tops meet,
Flowers and grass spring 'neath one's feet;
There was naught above me, naught below,
My childhood had not learned to know:
For, what are the voices of birds
—Ay, and of beasts,—but words, our words,
Only so much more sweet?
The knowledge of that with my life begun.
But I had so near made out the sun,
And counted your stars, the seven and one,
Like the fingers of my hand:
Nay, I could all but understand
Wherefore through heaven the white moon ranges;
And just when out of her soft fifty changes
No unfamiliar face might overlook me—
Suddenly God took me.

*[*PIPPA *passes.*

Mon. [*Springing up.*] My people—one and all—all—within there! Gag this villain—tie him hand and foot! He dares .. I know not half he dares—but remove him—quick! *Miserere mei, Domine!* Quick. I say!

PIPPA'S *Chamber again. She enters it.*

The bee with his comb,
The mouse at her dray,
The grub in his tomb,
While winter away;
But the fire-fly and hedge-shrew and lob-worm, I
      pray,
How fare they?
Ha, ha, thanks for your counsel, my Zanze!
"Feast upon lampreys, quaff Breganze"—
The summer of life so easy to spend,
And care for to-morrow so soon put away!
But winter hastens at summer's end,
And fire-fly, hedge-shrew, lob-worm, pray,
How fare they?
No bidding me then to . . . what did Zanze say?
"Pare your nails pearlwise, get your small feet shoes
More like" . . . (what said she?)—"and less like
      canoes!"
How pert that girl was!—would I be those pert
Impudent staring women! It had done me,
However, surely no such mighty hurt
To learn his name who passed that jest upon me:
No foreigner, that I can recollect,
Came, as she says, a month since, to inspect
Our silk-mills—none with blue eyes and thick rings
Of raw-silk-colored hair, at all events.
Well, if old Luca keep his good intents,

We shall do better, see what next year brings!
I may buy shoes, my Zanze, not appear
More destitute than you perhaps next year!
Bluph . . . something! I had caught the uncouth
    name
But for Monsignor's people's sudden clatter
Above us—bound to spoil such idle chatter
As ours: it were indeed a serious matter
If silly talk like ours should put to shame
The pious man, the man devoid of blame,
The . . . ah but—ah but, all the same,
No mere mortal has a right
To carry that exalted air;
Best people are not angels quite:
While—not the worst of people's doings scare
The devil; so there 's that proud look to spare!
   Which is mere counsel to myself, mind! for
I have just been the holy Monsignor:
And I was you too, Luigi's gentle mother,
And you too, Luigi!—how that Luigi started
Out of the turret—doubtlessly departed
On some good errand or another,
For he passed just now in a traveller's trim,
And the sullen company that prowled
About his path, I noticed, scowled
As if they had lost a prey in him.
And I was Jules the sculptor's bride,

And I was Ottima beside,
And now what am I?—tired of fooling.
Day for folly, night for schooling!
New year's day is over and spent,
Ill or well, I must be content.

　Even my lily 's asleep, I vow:
Wake up—here 's a friend I've plucked you!
Call this flower a heart's-ease now!
Something rare, let me instruct you,
Is this, with petals triply swollen,
Three times spotted, thrice the pollen;
While the leaves and parts that witness
Old proportions and their fitness,
Here remain unchanged, unmoved now;
Call this pampered thing improved now!
Suppose there 's a king of the flowers
And a girl-show held in his bowers—
"Look ye, buds, this growth of ours,"
Says he, "Zanze from the Brenta,
I have made her gorge polenta
Till both cheeks are near as bouncing
As her . . . name there 's no pronouncing!
See this heightened color too,
For she swilled Breganze wine
Till her nose turned deep carmine;
'T was but white when wild she grew.
And only by this Zanze's eyes

Of which we could not change the size,
The magnitude of all achieved
Otherwise, may be perceived."

Oh what a drear dark close to my poor day!
How could that red sun drop in that black cloud?
Ah Pippa, morning's rule is moved away,
Dispensed with, never more to be allowed!
Day's turn is over, now arrives the night's.
Oh lark, be day's apostle
To mavis, merle and throstle,
Bid them their betters jostle
From day and its delights!
But at night, brother owlet, over the woods,
Toll the world to thy chantry;
Sing to the bats' sleek sisterhoods
Full complines with gallantry:
Then, owls and bats,
Cowls and twats,
Monks and nuns, in a cloister's moods,
Adjourn to the oak-stump pantry!
              [*After she has begun to undress herself.*
Now, one thing I should like to really know:
How near I ever might approach all these
I only fancied being, this long day:
—Approach, I mean, so as to touch them, so
As to . . . in some way . . . move them—if you please,

Do good or evil to them some slight way.
For instance, if I wind
Silk to-morrow, my silk may bind

> [*Sitting on the bedside*

And border Ottima's cloak's hem.
Ah me, and my important part with them,
This morning's hymn half promised when I rose!
True in some sense or other, I suppose.

> [*As she lies down*

God bless me! I can pray no more to-night.
No doubt, some way or other, hymns say right.

All service ranks the same with God—
With God, whose puppets, best and worst,
Are we; there is no last nor first.

> [*She sleeps*

IN A BALCONY

PERSONS

NORBERT. THE QUEEN.
CONSTANCE. CONSTANCE AND NORBERT.

Norbert. Now!
Constance. Not now!
Nor. Give me them again, those hands;
Put them upon my forehead, how it throbs!

Press them before my eyes, the fire comes through!
You cruellest, you dearest in the world,
Let me! The Queen must grant whate'er I ask—
How can I gain you and not ask the Queen?
There she stays waiting for me, here stand you;
Sometime or other this was to be asked;
Now is the one time—what I ask, I gain:
Let me ask now, Love!

    Con.   Do, and ruin us!

   Nor. Let it be now, Love! All my soul breaks
     forth.

How I do love you! Give my love its way!
A man can have but one life and one death,
One heaven, one hell. Let me fulfil my fate—
Grant me my heaven now! Let me know you mine,
Prove you mine, write my name upon your brow,
Hold you and have you, and then die away,
If God please, with completion in my soul!

   Con. I am not yours then? How content this
     man!

I am not his—who change into himself,
Have passed into his heart and beat its beats,
Who give my hands to him, my eyes, my hair,
Give all that was of me away to him—
So well, that now, my spirit turned his own,
Takes part with him against the woman here,
Bids him not stumble at so mere a straw

As caring that the world be cognizant
How he loves her and how she worships him.
You have this woman, not as yet that world.
Go on, I bid, nor stop to care for me
By saving what I cease to care about,
The courtly name and pride of circumstance—
The name you 'll pick up and be cumbered with
Just for the poor parade's sake, nothing more;
Just that the world may slip from under you—
Just that the world may cry, "So much for him—
The man predestined to the heap of crowns:
There goes his chance of winning one, at last!"

   Nor. The world!

   Con. You love it! Love me quite as well,
And see if I shall pray for this in vain!
Why must you ponder what it knows or thinks?

   Nor. You pray for—what, in vain?

   Con.   Oh my heart's heart,
How I do love you, Norbert! That is right:
But listen, or I take my hands away!
You say, "Let it be now:" you would go now
And tell the Queen, perhaps six steps from us,
You love me—so you do, thank God!

   Nor.   Thank God!

   Con. Yes, Norbert,—but you fain would tell your
     love,
And, what succeeds the telling, ask of her

My hand. Now take this rose and look at it,
Listening to me. You are the minister,
The Queen's first favorite, nor without a cause,
To-night completes your wonderful year's-work
(This palace-feast is held to celebrate)
Made memorable by her life's success,
The junction of two crowns, on her sole head,
Her house had only dream of anciently:
That this mere dream is grown a stable truth,
To-night's feast makes authentic. Whose the praise?
Whose genius, patience, energy, achieved
What turned the many heads and broke the hearts?
You are the fate, your minute 's in the heaven,
Next comes the Queen's turn. "Name your own re-
          ward!"
With leave to clench the past, chain the outcome,
Put out an arm and touch and take the sun
And fix it ever full-faced on your earth,
Possess yourself supremely of her life,—
You choose the single thing she will not grant;
Nay, very declaration of which choice
Will turn the scale and neutralize your work:
At best she will forgive you, if she can.
You think I 'll let you choose—her cousin's hand?

   Nor. Wait. First, do you retain your old belief
The Queen is generous,—nay, is just?

   Con. There, there!

So men make women love them, while they know
No more of women's hearts than . . . look you here,
You that are just and generous beside.
Make it your own case! For example now,
I 'll say—I let you kiss me, hold my hands—
Why? do you know why? I 'll instruct you, then—
The kiss, because you have a name at court;
This hand and this, that you may shut in each
A jewel, if you please to pick up such.
That 's horrible? Apply it to the Queen—
Suppose I am the Queen to whom you speak.
"I was a nameless man; you needed me:
Why did I proffer you my aid? there stood
A certain pretty cousin at your side.
Why did I make such common cause with you?
Access to her had not been easy else.
You give my labor here abundant praise?
'Faith, labor, which she overlooked, grew play.
How shall your gratitude discharge itself?
Give me her hand!"

   Nor.   And still I urge the same.
Is the Queen just? just—generous or no!

   Con. Yes, just. You love a rose: no harm in that:
But was it for the rose's sake or mine
You put it in your bosom? mine, you said—
Then, mine you still must say or else be false.
You told the Queen you served her for herself;

If so, to serve her was to serve yourself,
She thinks, for all your unbelieving face!
I know her. In the hall, six steps from us,
One sees the twenty pictures: there 's a life
Better than life, and yet no life at all.
Conceive her born in such a magic dome,
Pictures all round her! why, she sees the world,
Can recognize its given things and facts,
The fight of giants or the feast of gods,
Sages in senate, beauties at the bath,
Chases and battles, the whole earth's display,
Landscape and sea-piece, down to flowers and fruit—
And who shall question that she knows them all,
In better semblance than the things outside?
Yet bring into the silent gallery
Some live thing to contrast in breath and blood,
Some lion, with the painted lion there—
You think she 'll understand composedly?
—Say, "that 's his fellow in the hunting-piece
Yonder, I 've turned to praise a hundred times?"
Not so. Her knowledge of our actual earth,
Its hopes and fears, concerns and sympathies,
Must be too far, too mediate, too unreal.
The real exists for us outside, not her:
How should it, with that life in these four walls,
That father and that mother, first to last
No father and no mother—friends, a heap,

Lovers, no lack—a husband in due time,
And every one of them alike a lie!
Things painted by a Rubens out of naught
Into what kindness, friendship, love should be;
All better, all more grandiose than the life,
Only no life; mere cloth and surface-paint,
You feel, while you admire. How should she feel?
Yet now that she has stood thus fifty years
The sole spectator in that gallery,
You think to bring this warm real struggling love
In to her of a sudden, and suppose
She 'll keep her state untroubled? Here 's the truth—
She 'll apprehend truth's value at a glance,
Prefer it to the pictured loyalty?
You only have to say, "So men are made,
For this they act; the thing has many names,
But this the right one: and now, Queen, be just!"
Your life slips back; you lose her at the word:
You do not even for amends gain me.
He will not understand! oh, Norbert, Norbert,
Do you not understand?

    Nor.   The Queen 's the Queen.
I am myself—no picture, but alive
In every nerve and every muscle, here
At the palace-window o'er the people's street,
As she in the gallery where the pictures glow:
The good of life is precious to us both.

She cannot love; what do I want with rule?
When first I saw your face a year ago
I knew my life's good, my soul heard one voice—
"The woman yonder, there 's no use of life
But just to obtain her! heap earth's woes in one
And bear them—make a pile of all earth's joys
And spurn them, as they help or help not this:
Only, obtain her!" How was it to be?
I found you were the cousin of the Queen;
I must then serve the Queen to get to you.
No other way. Suppose there had been one,
And I, by saying prayers to some white star
With promise of my body and my soul,
Might gain you,—should I pray the star or no?
Instead, there was the Queen to serve! I served,
Helped, did what other servants failed to do.
Neither she sought nor I declared my end.
Her good is hers, my recompense be mine,—
I therefore name you as that recompense.
She dreamed that such a thing could never be?
Let her wake now. She thinks there was more cause
In love of power, high fame, pure loyalty?
Perhaps she fancies men wear out their lives
Chasing such shades. Then, I 've a fancy too;
I worked because I want you with my soul:
I therefore ask your hand. Let it be now!

  Con. Had I not loved you from the very first,

Were I not yours, could we not steal out thus
So wickedly, so wildly, and so well,
You might become impatient. What 's conceived
Of us without here, by the folk within?
Where are you now? immersed in cares of state—
Where am I now? intent on festal robes—
We two, embracing under death's spread hand!
What was this thought for, what that scruple of yours
Which broke the council up?—to bring about
One minute's meeting in the corridor!
And then the sudden sleights, strange secrecies,
Complots inscrutable, deep telegraphs,
Long-planned chance-meetings, hazards of a look,
"Does she know? does she not know? saved or lost?"
A year of this compression's ecstasy
All goes for nothing! you would give this up
For the old way, the open way, the world's,
His way who beats, and his who sells his wife!
What tempts you?—their notorious happiness
Makes you ashamed of ours? The best you 'll gain
Will be—the Queen grants all that you require,
Concedes the cousin, rids herself of you
And me at once, and gives us ample leave
To live like our five hundred happy friends.
The world will show us with officious hand
Our chamber-entry, and stand sentinel
Where we so oft have stolen across its traps?

Get the world's warrant, ring the falcons' feet,
And make it duty to be bold and swift,
Which long ago was nature. Have it so!
We never hawked by rights till flung from fist?
Oh, the man's thought! no woman 's such a fool.

  Nor. Yes, the man's thought and my thought,
      which is more—
One made to love you, let the world take note!
Have I done worthy work? be love's the praise,
Though hampered by restrictions, barred against
By set forms, blinded by forced secrecies!
Set free my love, and see what love can do
Shown in my life—what work will spring from that!
The world is used to have its business done
On other grounds, find great effects produced
For power's sake, fame's sake, motives in men's
      mouth.
So, good: but let my low ground shame their high!
Truth is the strong thing. Let man's life be true!
And love 's the truth of mine. Time prove the rest!
I choose to wear you stamped all over me,
Your name upon my forehead and my breast,
You, from the sword's blade to the ribbon's edge,
That men may see, all over, you in me—
That pale loves may die out of their pretence
In face of mine, shames thrown on love fall off.
Permit this, Constance! Love has been so long

Subdued in me, eating me through and through,
That now 't is all of me and must have way.
Think of my work, that chaos of intrigues,
Those hopes and fears, surprises and delays,
That long endeavor, earnest, patient, slow,
Trembling at last to its assured result:
Then think of this revulsion! I resume
Life after death, (it is no less than life,
After such long unlovely laboring days,)
And liberate to beauty life's great need
O' the beautiful, which, while it prompted work,
Suppressed itself erewhile. This eve 's the time,
This eve intense with yon first trembling star
We seem to pant and reach; scarce aught between
The earth that rises and the heaven that bends;
All nature self-abandoned, every tree
Flung as it will, pursuing its own thoughts
And fixed so, every flower and every weed,
No pride, no shame, no victory, no defeat;
All under God, each measured by itself.
These statues round us stand abrupt, distinct,
The strong in strength, the weak in weakness fixed,
The Muse forever wedded to her lyre,
Nymph to her fawn, and Silence to her rose:
See God's approval on his universe!
Let us do so—aspire to live as these
In harmony with truth, ourselves being true!

Take the first way, and let the second come!
My first is to possess myself of you;
The music sets the march-step—forward, then!
And there 's the Queen, I go to claim you of,
The world to witness, wonder and applaud.
Our flower of life breaks open. No delay!

  Con.   And so shall we be ruined, both of us,
Norbert, I know her to the skin and bone:
You do not know her, were not born to it,
To feel what she can see or cannot see.
Love, she is generous,—ay, despite your smile,
Generous as you are: for, in that thin frame
Pain-twisted, punctured through and through with
     cares,
There lived a lavish soul until it starved,
Debarred of healthy food. Look to the soul—
Pity that, stoop to that, ere you begin
(The true man's-way) on justice and your rights,
Exactions and acquittance of the past!
Begin so—see what justice she will deal!
We women hate a debt as men a gift.
Suppose her some poor keeper of a school
Whose business is to sit through summer months
And dole out children leave to go and play,
Herself superior to such lightness—she
In the arm-chair's state and pædagogic pomp—
To the life, the laughter, sun and youth, outside:

We wonder such a face looks black on us?
I do not bid you wake her tenderness,
(That were vain truly—none is left to wake,)
But, let her think her justice is engaged
To take the shape of tenderness, and mark
If she 'll not coldly pay its warmest debt!
Does she love me, I ask you? not a whit:
Yet, thinking that her justice was engaged
To help a kinswoman, she took me up—
Did more on that bare ground than other loves
Would do on greater argument. For me,
I have no equivalent of such cold kind
To pay her with, but love alone to give
If I give anything. I give her love:
I feel I ought to help her, and I will.
So, for her sake, as yours, I tell you twice
That women hate a debt as men a gift.
If I were you, I could obtain this grace—
Could lay the whole I did to love's account,
Nor yet be very false as courtiers go—
Declaring my success was recompense;
It would be so, in fact: what were it else?
And then, once loose her generosity,—
Oh, how I see it! then, were I but you
To turn it, let it seem to move itself,
And make it offer what I really take,
Accepting just, in the poor cousin's hand,

Her value as the next thing to the Queen's—
Since none love Queens directly, none dare that,
And a thing's shadow or a name's mere echo
Suffices those who miss the name and thing!
You pick up just a ribbon she has worn,
To keep in proof how near her breath you came.
Say, I 'm so near I seem a piece of her—
Ask for me that way—(oh, you understand,)
You 'd find the same gift yielded with a grace,
Which, if you make the least show to extort . . .
—You 'll see! and when you have ruined both of us,
Dissertate on the Queen's ingratitude!

    Nor.   Then, if I turn it that way, you consent?
'T is not my way; I have more hope in truth:
Still, if you won't have truth—why, this indeed,
Were scarcely false, as I 'd express the sense,
Will you remain here?

    Con.   O best heart of mine,
How I have loved you! then, you take my way?
Are mine as you have been her minister,
Work out my thought, give it effect for me,
Paint plain my poor conceit and make it serve?
I owe that withered woman everything—
Life, fortune, you, remember! Take my part—
Help me to pay her! Stand upon your rights?
You, with my rose, my hands, my heart on you?
Your rights are mine—you have no rights but mine.

Nor. Remain here. How you know me!

Con.   Ah, but still—

[*He breaks from her; she remains. Dance-music from within.*

(*Enter the* QUEEN)

Queen. Constance? She is here as he said. Speak
   quick!
Is it so? Is it true or false? One word!

Con. True.

Queen. Mercifullest Mother, thanks to thee!

Con. Madam?

Queen. I love you, Constance, from my soul.
Now say once more, with any words you will,
'T is true, all true, as true as that I speak.

Con. Why should you doubt it?

Queen.   Ah, why doubt? why doubt?
Dear, make me see it! Do you see it so?
None see themselves; another sees them best.
You say "why doubt it?"—you see him and me.
It is because the Mother has such grace
That if we had but faith—wherein we fail—
Whate'er we yearn for would be granted us;
Yet still we let our whims prescribe despair,
Our fancies thwart and cramp our will and power,
And while accepting life, abjure its use.

Constance, I had abjured the hope of love
And being loved, as truly as yon palm
The hope of seeing Egypt from that plot.

   Con. Heaven!

   Queen. But it was so, Constance, it was so!
Men say—or do men say it? fancies say—
"Stop here, your life is set, you are grown old.
Too late—no love for you, too late for love—
Leave love to girls. Be queen: let Constance love!"
One takes the hint—half meets it like a child,
Ashamed at any feelings that oppose.
"Oh love, true, never think of love again!
I am a queen: I rule, not love, forsooth."
So it goes on; so a face grows like this,
Hair like this hair, poor arms as lean as these,
Till,—nay, it does not end so, I thank God!

   Con. I cannot understand—

   Queen.   The happier you!
Constance, I know not how it is with men:
For women (I am a woman now like you)
There is no good of life but love—but love!
What else looks good, is some shade flung from love;
Love gilds it, gives it worth. Be warned by me,
Never you cheat yourself one instant! Love,
Give love, ask only love, and leave the rest!
O Constance, how I love you!

   Con.   I love you.

Queen. I do believe that all is come through you.
I took you to my heart to keep it warm
When the last chance of love seemed dead in me;
I thought your fresh youth warmed my withered
      heart.
Oh, I am very old now, am I not?
Not so! it is true and it shall be true!

   Con. Tell it me: let me judge if true or false.

   Queen. Ah, but I fear you! you will look at me
And say, "she 's old, she 's grown unlovely quite
Who ne'er was beauteous: men want beauty still."
Well, so I feared—the curse! so I felt sure!

   Con. Be calm. And now you feel not sure, you
      say?

   Queen. Constance, he came,—the coming was not
      strange—
Do not I stand and see men come and go?
I turned a half-look from my pedestal
Where I grow marble—"one young man the more!
He will love some one; that is naught to me:
What would he with my marble stateliness?"
Yet this seemed somewhat worse than heretofore;
The man more gracious, youthful, like a god,
And I still older, with less flesh to change—
We two those dear extremes that long to touch.
It seemed still harder when he first began
To labor at those state-affairs, absorbed

The old way for the old end—interest.
Oh, to live with a thousand beating hearts
Around you, swift eyes, serviceable hands,
Professing they 've no care but for your cause,
Thought but to help you, love but for yourself,—
And you the marble statue all the time
They praise and point at as preferred to life,
Yet leave for the first breathing woman's smile,
First dancer's, gypsy's, or street baladine's!
Why, how I have ground my teeth to hear men's
    speech
Stifled for fear it should alarm my ear,
Their gait subdued lest step should startle me,
Their eyes declined, such queendom to respect,
Their hands alert, such treasure to preserve,
While not a man of them broke rank and spoke,
Wrote me a vulgar letter all of love,
Or caught my hand and pressed it like a hand!
There have been moments, if the sentinel
Lowering his halbert to salute the queen,
Had flung it brutally and clasped my knees,
I would have stooped and kissed him with my soul.
    Con. Who could have comprehended?
    Queen.   Ah, who—who?
Why, no one, Constance, but this one who did.
Not they, not you, not I. Even now perhaps
It comes too late—would you but tell the truth.

Con. I wait to tell it.

Queen.   Well, you see, he came.
Out faced the others, did a work this year
Exceeds in value all was ever done,
You know—it is not I who say it—all
Say it. And so (a second pang and worse)
I grew aware not only of what he did,
But why so wondrously. Oh, never work
Like his was done for work's ignoble sake—
Souls need a finer aim to light and lure!
I felt, I saw, he loved—loved somebody.
And Constance, my dear Constance, do you know,
I did believe this while 't was you he loved.

Con. Me, madam?

Queen.   It did seem to me, your face
Met him where'er he looked: and whom but you
Was such a man to love? It seemed to me,
You saw he loved you, and approved his love,
And both of you were in intelligence.
You could not loiter in that garden, step
Into this balcony, but I straight was stung
And forced to understand. It seemed so true,
So right, so beautiful, so like you both,
That all this work should have been done by him
Not for the vulgar hope of recompense,
But that at last—suppose, some night like this—
Borne on to claim his due reward of me,

He might say, "Give her hand and pay me so."
And I (O Constance, you shall love me now!)
I thought, surmounting all the bitterness,
—"And he shall have it. I will make her blest,
My flower of youth, my woman's self that was,
My happiest woman's self that might have been!
These two shall have their joy and leave me here."
Yes—yes!

    Con. Thanks!

    Queen.   And the word was on my lips
When he burst in upon me. I looked to hear
A mere calm statement of his just desire
For payment of his labor. When—O heaven,
How can I tell you? lightning on my eyes
And thunder in my ears proved that first word
Which told 't was love of me, of me, did all—
He loved me—from the first step to the last,
Loved me!

    Con. You hardly saw, scarce heard him speak
Of love: what if you should mistake?

    Queen.   No, no—
No mistake! Ha, there shall be no mistake!
He had not dared to hint the love he felt—
You were my reflex—(how I understood!)
He said you were the ribbon I had worn,
He kissed my hand, he looked into my eyes,
And love, love came at end of every phrase.

Love is begun; this much is come to pass:
The rest is easy. Constance, I am yours!
I will learn, I will place my life on you,
Teach me but how to keep what I have won!
Am I so old? This hair was early gray;
But joy ere now has brought hair brown again,
And joy will bring the cheek's red back, I feel.
I could sing once too; that was in my youth.
Still, when men paint me, they declare me ... yes,
Beautiful—for the last French painter did!
I know they flatter somewhat; you are frank—
I trust you. How I loved you from the first!
Some queens would hardly seek a cousin out
And set her by their side to take the eye:
I must have felt that good would come from you.
I am not generous—like him—like you!
But he is not your lover after all:
It was not you he looked at. Saw you him?
You have not been mistaking words or looks?
He said you were the reflex of myself.
And yet he is not such a paragon
To you, to younger women who may choose
Among a thousand Norberts. Speak the truth!
You know you never named his name to me:
You know, I cannot give him up—ah God,
Not up now, even to you!

 Con.   Then calm yourself

Queen.   See, I am old—look here, you happy girl!
I will not play the fool, deceive—ah, whom?
'T is all gone: put your cheek beside my cheek
And what a contrast does the moon behold!
But then I set my life upon one chance,
The last chance and the best—am *I* not left,
My soul, myself? All women love great men
If young or old; it is in all the tales:
Young beauties love old poets who can love—
Why should not he, the poems in my soul,
The passionate faith, the pride of sacrifice,
Life-long, death-long? I throw them at his feet.
Who cares to see the fountain's very shape,
Whether it be a Triton's or a Nymph's
That pours the foam, makes rainbows all around?
You could not praise indeed the empty conch;
But I 'll pour floods of love and hide myself.
How I will love him! Cannot men love love?
Who was a queen and loved a poet once
Humpbacked, a dwarf? ah, women can do that!
Well, but men too; at least, they tell you so.
They love so many women in their youth,
And even in age they all love whom they please;
And yet the best of them confide to friends
That 't is not beauty makes the lasting love—
They spend a day with such and tire the next:
They like soul,—well then, they like phantasy,

Novelty even. Let us confess the truth,
Horrible though it be, that prejudice,
Prescription . . . curses! they will love a queen.
They will, they do: and will not, does not—he?

   Con. How can he? You are wedded: 't is a name
We know, but still a bond. Your rank remains,
His rank remains. How can he, nobly souled
As you believe and I incline to think,
Aspire to be your favorite, shame and all?

   Queen. Hear her! There, there now—could she
      love like me?
What did I say of smooth-cheeked youth and grace?
See all it does or could do! so youth loves!
Oh, tell him, Constance, you could never do
What I will—you, it was not born in! I
Will drive these difficulties far and fast
As yonder mists curdling before the moon.
I 'll use my light too, gloriously retrieve
My youth from its enforced calamity,
Dissolve that hateful marriage, and be his,
His own in the eyes alike of God and man.

   Con. You will do—dare do . . . pause on what
      you say!

   Queen. Hear her! I thank you, sweet, for that
      surprise.
You have the fair face: for the soul, see mine!
I have the strong soul: let me teach you, here.

I think I have borne enough and long enough,
And patiently enough, the world remarks,
To have my own way now, unblamed by all.
It does so happen (I rejoice for it)
This most unhoped-for issue cuts the knot.
There 's not a better way of settling claims
Than this; God sends the accident express:
And were it for my subjects' good, no more,
'T were best thus ordered. I am thankful now,
Mute, passive, acquiescent. I receive,
And bless God simply, or should almost fear
To walk so smoothly to my ends at last.
Why, how I baffle obstacles, spurn fate!
How strong I am! Could Norbert see me now!
   Con. Let me consider. It is all too strange.
   Queen. You, Constance, learn of me; do you, like
       me!
You are young, beautiful: my own, best girl,
You will have many lovers, and love one—
Light hair, not hair like Norbert's, to suit yours,
Taller than he is, since yourself are tall.
Love him, like me! Give all away to him;
Think never of yourself; throw by your pride,
Hope, fear,—your own good as you saw it once,
And love him simply for his very self.
Remember, I (and what am I to you?)
Would give up all for one, leave throne, lose life.

Do all but just unlove him! He loves me.

  Con. He shall.

  Queen.   You, step inside my inmost heart!

Give me your own heart: let us have one heart!

I 'll come to you for counsel; "this he says,

This he does; what should this amount to, pray?

Beseech you, change it into current coin!

Is that worth kisses? Shall I please him there?"

And then we 'll speak in turn of you—what else?

Your love, according to your beauty's worth,

For you shall have some noble love, all gold:

Whom choose you? we will get him at your choice.

—Constance, I leave you. Just a minute since,

I felt as I must die or be alone

Breathing my soul into an ear like yours:

Now, I would face the world with my new life,

Wear my new crown. I 'll walk around the rooms,

And then come back and tell you how it feels.

How soon a smile of God can change the world!

How we are made for happiness—how work

Grows play, adversity a winning fight!

True, I have lost so many years: what then?

Many remain: God has been very good.

You, stay here! 'T is as different from dreams,

From the mind's cold calm estimate of bliss,

As these stone statues from the flesh and blood.

The comfort thou hast caused mankind, God's moon!

[*She goes out, leaving* CONSTANCE. *Dance-music from
within.*

(NORBERT *enters.*)

   Nor. Well? we have but one minute and one word!
   Con. I am yours, Norbert!
   Nor.   Yes, mine.
   Con.   Not till now!
You were mine. Now I give myself to you.
   Nor. Constance?
   Con. Your own! I know the thriftier way
Of giving—haply, 't is the wiser way.
Meaning to give a treasure, I might dole
Coin after coin out (each, as that were all,
With a new largess still at each despair)
And force you keep in sight the deed, preserve
Exhaustless till the end my part and yours,
My giving and your taking; both our joys
Dying together. Is it the wiser way?
I choose the simpler; I give all at once.
Know what you have to trust to, trade upon!
Use it, abuse it,—anything but think
Hereafter, "Had I known she loved me so,
And what my means, I might have thriven with it."
This is your means. I give you all myself.
   Nor. I take you and thank God.

Con.   Look on through years!
We cannot kiss, a second day like this;
Else were this earth no earth.
    Nor.   With this day's heat
We shall go on through years of cold.
    Con.   So, best!
—I try to see those years—I think I see.
You walk quick and new warmth comes; you look
        back
And lay all to the first glow—not sit down
Forever brooding on a day like this
While seeing embers whiten and love die.
Yes, love lives best in its effect; and mine,
Full in its own life, yearns to live in yours.
    Nor. Just so. I take and know you all at once.
Your soul is disengaged so easily.
Your face is there, I know you; give me time,
Let me be proud and think you shall know me.
My soul is slower: in a life I roll
The minute out whereto you condense yours—
The whole slow circle round you I must move,
To be just you. I look to a long life
To decompose this minute, prove its worth.
'T is the sparks' long succession one by one
Shall show you, in the end, what fire was crammed
In that mere stone you struck: how could you know,
If it lay ever unproved in your sight,

As now my heart lies? your own warmth would hide
Its coldness, were it cold.

  Con.   But how prove, how?

  Nor.   Prove in my life, you ask?

  Con.   Quick, Norbert—how?

  Nor.   That 's easy told. I count life just a stuff
To try the soul's strength on, educe the man.
Who keeps one end in view makes all things serve
As with the body—he who hurls a lance
Or heaps up stone on stone, shows strength alike:
So must I seize and task all means to prove
And show this soul of mine, you crown as yours,
And justify us both.

  Con.   Could you write books,
Paint pictures! One sits down in poverty
And writes or paints, with pity for the rich.

  Nor.   And loves one's painting and one's writing,
    then.
And not one's mistress! All is best, believe,
And we best as no other than we are.
We live, and they experiment on life—
Those poets, painters, all who stand aloof
To overlook the farther. Let us be
The thing they look at! I might take your face
And write of it and paint it—to what end?
For whom? what pale dictatress in the air
Feeds, smiling sadly, her fine ghost-like form

With earth's real blood and breath, the beauteous life
She makes despised forever? You are mine,
Made for me, not for others in the world,
Nor yet for that which I should call my art,
The cold calm power to see how fair you look.
I come to you; I leave you not, to write
Or paint. You are, I am: let Rubens there
Paint us!

   Con.   So, best!

   Nor.   I understand your soul,
You live, and rightly sympathize with life,
With action, power, success. This way is straight;
And time were short beside, to let me change
The craft my childhood learnt: my craft shall serve
Men set me here to subjugate, enclose,
Manure their barren lives, and force thence fruit
First for themselves, and afterward for me
In the due tithe; the task of some one soul,
Through ways of work appointed by the world.
I am not bid create—men see no star
Transfiguring my brow to warrant that—
But find and bind and bring to bear their wills,
So I began: to-night sees how I end.
What if it see, too, power's first outbreak here
Amid the warmth, surprise and sympathy,
And instincts of the heart that teach the head?
What if the people have discerned at length

The dawn of the next nature, novel brain
Whose will they venture in the place of theirs,
Whose work, they trust, shall find them as novel **ways**
To untried heights which yet he only sees?
I felt it when you kissed me. See this Queen,
This people—in our phrase this mass of men—
See how the mass lies passive to my hand
Now that my hand is plastic, with you by
To make the muscles iron! Oh, an end
Shall crown this issue as this crowns the first!
My will be on the people! then, the strain,
The grappling of the potter with his clay,
The long uncertain struggle,—the success
And consummation of the spirit-work,
Some vase shape to the curl of the god's lip,
While rounded fair for human sense to see
The Graces in a dance men recognize
With turbulent applause and laughs of heart!
So triumph ever shall renew itself;
Ever shall end in efforts higher yet,
Ever begin . . .

   Con.   I ever helping?

   Nor.   Thus!

      (*As he embraces her, the* QUEEN *enters.*)

   Con. Hist, madam! So have I performed **my part.**
You see your gratitude's true decency,

Norbert? A little slow in seeing it!
Begin, to end the sooner! What 's a kiss?
 Nor. Constance?
 Con.   Why, must I teach it you **again**?
You want a witness to your dulness, sir?
What was I saying these ten minutes long?
Then I repeat—when some young handsome **man**
Like you has acted out a part like yours,
Is pleased to fall in love with one beyond,
So very far beyond him, as he says—
So hopelessly in love that but to speak
Would prove him mad,—he thinks judiciously,
And makes some insignificant good soul,
Like me, his friend, adviser, confidant,
And very stalking-horse to cover him
In following after what he dares not face—
When his end 's gained—(sir, do you understand?)
When she, he dares not face, has loved him first,
—May I not say so, madam?—tops his hope,
And overpasses so his wildest dream,
With glad consent of all, and most of her
The confidant who brought the same about—
Why, in the moment when such joy explodes,
I do hold that the merest gentleman
Will not start rudely from the stalking-horse,
Dismiss it with a "There, enough of you!"
Forget it, show his back unmannerly;

But like a liberal heart will rather turn
And say, "A tingling time of hope was ours;
Betwixt the fears and falterings, we two lived
A chanceful time in waiting for the prize:
The confidant, the Constance, served not ill.
And though I shall forget her in good time,
Her use being answered now, as reason bids,
Nay as herself bids from her heart of hearts,—
Still, she has rights, the first thanks go to her,
The first good praise goes to the prosperous tool,
And the first—which is the last—rewarding kiss."
  Nor. Constance, it is a dream—ah, see, you smile!
  Con. So, now his part being properly performed,
Madam, I turn to you and finish mine
As duly; I do justice in my turn.
Yes, madam, he has loved you—long and well;
He could not hope to tell you so—'t was I
Who served to prove your soul accessible,
I led his thoughts on, drew them to their place
When they had wandered else into despair,
And kept love constant toward its natural aim.
Enough, my part is played; you stoop half-way
And meet us royally and spare our fears:
'T is like yourself. He thanks you, so do I.
Take him—with my full heart! my work is praised
By what comes of it. Be you happy, both!
Yourself—the only one on earth who can—

Do all for him, much more than a mere heart
Which though warm is not useful in its warmth
As the silk vesture of a queen! fold that
Around him gently, tenderly. For him—
For him,—he knows his own part!

Nor.   Have you done?
I take the jest at last. Should I speak now?
Was yours the wager, Constance, foolish child,
Or did you but accept it? Well—at least
You lose by it.

Con.   Nay, madam, 't is your turn!
Restrain him still from speech a little more,
And make him happier as more confident!
Pity him, madam, he is timid yet!
Mark, Norbert! Do not shrink now! Here I yield
My whole right in you to the Queen, observe!
With her go put in practice the great schemes
You teem with, follow the career else closed—
Be all you cannot be except by her!
Behold her!—Madam, say for pity's sake
Anything—frankly say you love him! Else
He 'll not believe it: there 's more earnest in
His fear than you conceive: I know the man!

Nor. I know the woman somewhat, and confess
I thought she had jested better: she begins
To overcharge her part. I gravely wait
Your pleasure, madam: where is my reward?

Queen. Norbert, this wild girl (whom I recognize
Scarce more than you do, in her fancy-fit,
Eccentric speech and variable mirth,
Not very wise perhaps and somewhat bold,
Yet suitable, the whole night's work being strange)
—May still be right: I may do well to speak
And make authentic what appears a dream
To even myself. For, what she says is true:
Yes, Norbert—what you spoke just now of love,
Devotion, stirred no novel sense in me,
But justified a warmth felt long before.
Yes, from the first—I loved you, I shall say:
Strange! but I do grow stronger, now 't is said.
Your courage helps mine: you did well to speak
To-night, the night that crowns your twelve-months'
        toil:
But still I had not waited to discern
Your heart so long, believe me! From the first
The source of so much zeal was almost plain,
In absence even of your own words just now
Which hazarded the truth.   'T is very strange,
But takes a happy ending—in your love
Which mine meets: be it so! as you choose me,
So I choose you.
    Nor.   And worthily you choose.
I will not be unworthy your esteem,
No, madam. I do love you; I will meet

Your nature, now I know it. This was well.
I see,—you dare and you are justified:
But none had ventured such experiment,
Less versed than you in nobleness of heart,
Less confident of finding such in me.
I joy that thus you test me ere you grant
The dearest, richest, beauteousest and best
Of women to my arms: 't is like yourself.
So—back again into my part's set words—
Devotion to the uttermost is yours,
But no, you cannot, madam, even you,
Create in me the love our Constance does.
Or—something truer to the tragic phrase—
Not yon magnolia-bell superb with scent
Invites a certain insect—that 's myself—
But the small eye-flower nearer to the ground.
I take this lady.

    Con.   Stay—not hers, the trap—
Stay, Norbert—that mistake were worst of all!
He is too cunning, madam! It was I,
I, Norbert, whc . . .

    Nor.   You, was it, Constance? Then,
But for the grace of this divinest hour
Which gives me you, I might not pardon here!
I am the Queen's; she only knows my brain:
She may experiment upon my heart
And I instruct her too by the result.

But you, Sweet, you who know me, who so long
Have told my heartbeats over, held my life
In those white hands of yours,—it is not well!

  Con. Tush! I have said it, did I not say it all?
The life, for her—the heartbeats, for her sake!

   Nor. Enough! my cheek grows red, I think. Your
      test?

There 's not the meanest woman in the world,
Not she I least could love in all the world,
Whom, did she love me, had love proved itself,
I dare insult as you insult me now.
Constance, I could say, if it must be said,
"Take back the soul you offer, I keep mine!"
But—"Take the soul still quivering on your hand,
The soul so offered, which I cannot use,
And, please you, give it to some playful friend,
For—what 's the trifle he requites me with?"
I, tempt a woman, to amuse a man,
That two may mock her heart if it succumb?
No: fearing God and standing 'neath his heaven,
I would not dare insult a woman so,
Were she the meanest woman in the world,
And he, I cared to please, ten emperors!

  Con. Norbert!

  Nor.   I love once as I live but once.
What case is this to think or talk about?
I love you. Would it mend the case at all

If such a step as this killed love in me?
Your part were done: account to God for it!
But mine—could murdered love get up again,
And kneel to whom you please to designate,
And make you mirth? It is too horrible.
You did not know this, Constance? now you know
That body and soul have each one life, but one:
And here 's my love, here, living, at your feet.

   Con. See the Queen! Norbert—this one more last
        word—

If thus you have taken jest for earnest—thus
Loved me in earnest . . .

   Nor.   Ah, no jest holds here!
Where is the laughter in which jests break up,
And what this horror that grows palpable?
Madam—why grasp you thus the balcony?
Have I done ill? Have I not spoken truth?
How could I other? Was it not your test,
To try me, what my love for Constance meant?
Madam, your royal soul itself approves,
The first, that I should choose thus! so one takes
A beggar,—asks him, what would buy his child?
And then approves the expected laugh of scorn
Returned as something noble from the rags.
Speak, Constance, I 'm the beggar! Ha, what 's this?
You two glare each at each like panthers now.
Constance, the world fades; only you stand there!

You did not, in to-night's wild whirl of things,
Sell me—your soul of souls, for any price?
No—no—'t is easy to believe in you!
Was it your love's mad trial to o'ertop
Mine by this vain self-sacrifice? well, still—
Though I might curse, I love you. I am love
And cannot change: love 's self is at your feet!

                                        [The QUEEN *goes out.*

   Con.   Feel my heart; let it die against your own!
   Nor.   Against my own. Explain not; let this be!
This is life's height.
   Con.   Yours, yours, yours!
   Nor.   You and I—
Why care by what meanders we are here
I' the centre of the labyrinth? Men have died
Trying to find this place, which we have found.
   Con.   Found, found!
   Nor.   Sweet, never fear what she can do!
We are past harm now.
   Con.   On the breast of God.
I thought of men—as if you were a man.
Tempting him with a crown!
   Nor.   This must end here:
It is too perfect.
   Con.   There 's the music stopped.
What measured heavy tread? It is one blaze
About me and within me.

Nor.   Oh, some death
Will run its sudden finger round this spark
And sever us from the rest!

Con.   And so do well.
Now the doors open,

Nor.   'T is the guard comes.

Con.   Kiss!

IDYLLS

PHEIDIPPIDES

Χαίρετε, νικῶμεν.

FIRST I salute this soil of the blessed, river and rock!
Gods of my birthplace, dæmons and heroes, honor to
    all!
Then I name thee, claim thee for our patron, co-equal
    in praise
—Ay, with Zeus the Defender, with Her of the ægis
    and spear!
Also, ye of the bow and the buskin, praised be your
    peer.
Now, henceforth and forever,—O latest to whom I
    upraise
Hand and heart and voice! For Athens, leave pasture
    and flock!
Present to help, potent to save, Pan—patron I call!

Archons of Athens, topped by the tettix, see, I return!
See, 't is myself here standing alive, no spectre that
    speaks!
Crowned with the myrtle, did you command me,
    Athens and you,

"Run, Pheidippides, run and race, reach Sparta for
    aid!

Persia has come, we are here, where is She?" Your
    command I obeyed,

Ran and raced: like stubble, some field which a fire
    runs through,

Was the space between city and city: two days, two
    nights did I burn

Over the hills, under the dales, down pits and up
    peaks,

Into their midst I broke: breath served but for "Persia
    has come!

Persia bids Athens proffer slaves'-tribute, water and
    earth;

Razed to the ground is Eretria—but Athens, shall
    Athens sink,

Drop into dust and die—the flower of Hellas utterly
    die,

Die, with the wide world spitting at Sparta, the stupid,
    the stander-by?

Answer me quick, what help, what hand do you stretch
    o'er destruction's brink?

How,—when? No care for my limbs!—there 's light-
    ning in all and some—

Fresh and fit your message to bear, once lips give it
    birth!"

O my Athens--Sparta love thee? Did Sparta re-
     spond?

Every face of her leered in a furrow of envy, mistrust,

Malice,—each eye of her gave me its glitter of grati-
     fied hate!

Gravely they turned to take counsel, to cast for ex-
     cuses. I stood

Quivering,—the limbs of me fretting as fire frets, an
     inch from dry wood:

"Persia has come, Athens asks aid, and still they de-
     bate?

Thunder, thou Zeus! Athene, are Spartans a quarry
     beyond

Swing of thy spear? Phoibos and Artemis, clang them
     'Ye must'!"

No bolt launched from Olumpos! Lo, their answer at
     last!

"Has Persia come,—does Athens ask aid, — may
     Sparta befriend?

Nowise precipitate judgment—too weighty the issue
     at stake!

Count we no time lost time which lags through respect
     to the gods!

Ponder that precept of old, 'No warfare, whatever the
     odds

In your favor, so long as the moon, half-orbed, is
     unable to take

Full-circle her state in the sky!' Already she rounds
    to it fast:
Athens must wait, patient as we—who judgment sus-
    pend."

Athens,—except for that sparkle,—thy name, I had
    mouldered to ash!
That sent a blaze through my blood; off, off and away
    was I back,
—Not one word to waste, one look to lose on the false
    and the vile!
Yet "O gods of my land!" I cried, as each hillock and
    plain,
Wood and stream, I knew, I named, rushing past them
    again,
"Have ye kept faith, proved mindful of honors we
    paid you erewhile?
Vain was the filleted victim, the fulsome libation!
    Too rash
Love in its choice, paid you so largely service so slack!

"Oak and olive and bay,—I bid you cease to en-
    wreathe
Brows made bold by your leaf! Fade at the Persian's
    foot,
You that, our patrons were pledged, should never
    adorn a slave!
Rather I hail thee, Parnes,—trust to thy wild waste
    tract!

Treeless, herbless, lifeless mountain! What matter if
     slacked
My speed may hardly be, for homage to crag and to
     cave
No deity deigns to drape with verdure? at least I can
     breathe,
Fear in thee no fraud from the blind, no lie from the
     mute!"

Such my cry as, rapid, I ran over Parnes' ridge;
Gully and gap I clambered and cleared till, sudden,
     a bar
Jutted, a stoppage of stone against me, blocking the
     way.
Right! for I minded the hollow to traverse, the fissure
     across:
"Where I could enter, there I depart by! Night in
     the fosse?
Athens to aid? Though the dive were through Erebos,
     thus I obey—
Out of the day dive, into the day as bravely arise!
     No bridge
Better!"—when—ha! what was it I came on, of won-
     ders that are?

There, in the cool of a cleft, sat he—majestical Pan!
Ivy drooped wanton, kissed his head, moss cushioned
     his hoof:

All the great god was good in the eyes grave-kindly—
the curl
Carved on the bearded cheek, amused at a mortal's
awe,
As, under the human trunk, the goat-thighs grand I
saw.
"Halt, Pheidippides!"—halt I did, my brain of a
whirl:
"Hither to me! Why pale in my presence?" he gracious began:
"How is it,—Athens, only in Hellas, holds me aloof?

"Athens, she only, rears me no fane, makes me no
feast!
Wherefore? Than I what godship to Athens more
helpful of old?
Go, bid Athens take heart, laugh Persia to scorn, have
faith
In the temples and tombs! Go, say to Athens, 'The
Goat-God saith:
When Persia—so much as strews not the soil—is cast
in the sea,
Then praise Pan who fought in the ranks with your
most and least,
Goat-thigh to greaved-thigh, made one cause with the
free and the bold!'

無

"Say Pan saith: 'Let this, foreshowing the place, be
    the pledge!'"

(Gay, the liberal hand held out this herbage I bear
—Fennel—I grasped it a-tremble with dew—whatever
    it bode)

"While, as for thee" . . . But enough! He was gone.
    If I ran hitherto—

Be sure that, the rest of my journey, I ran no longer,
    but flew.

Parnes to Athens—earth no more, the air was my
    road:

Here am I back. Praise Pan, we stand no more on the
    razor's edge!

Pan for Athens, Pan for me! I too have a guerdon
    rare!

Then spoke Miltiades. "And thee, best runner of
    Greece,

Whose limbs did duty indeed,—what gift is promised
    thyself?

Tell it us straightway,—Athens the mother demands
    of her son!"

Rosily blushed the youth: he paused: but, lifting at
    length

His eyes from the ground, it seemed as he gathered
    the rest of his strength

Into the utterance—"Pan spoke thus: 'For what thou
    hast done

Count on a worthy reward!   Henceforth be allowed
    the release

From the racer's toil, no vulgar reward in praise or in
    pelf!'

"I am bold to believe, Pan means reward the most to
    my mind!

Fight I shall, with our foremost, wherever this fennel
    may grow,—

Pound—Pan helping us—Persia to dust, and, under
    the deep,

Whelm her away forever; and then,—no Athens to
    save,—

Marry a certain maid, I know keeps faith to the
    brave,—

Hie to my house and home: and, when my children
    shall creep

Close to my knees,—recount how the God was awful
    yet kind,

Promised their sire reward to the full—rewarding him
    —so!"

Unforeseeing one!   Yes, he fought on the Marathon
    day:

So, when Persia was dust, all cried "To Akropolis!

Run, Pheidippides, one race more! the meed is thy
    due!
'Athens is saved, thank Pan,' go shout!" He flung
    down his shield,
Ran like fire once more: and the space 'twixt the
    Fennel-field
And Athens was stubble again, a field which a fire
    runs through,
Till in he broke: "Rejoice, we conquer!" Like wine
    through clay,
Joy in his blood bursting his heart, he died—the bliss!

So, to this day, when friend meets friend, the word of
    salute
Is still "Rejoice!"—his word which brought rejoicing
    indeed.
So is Pheidippides happy forever,—the noble strong
    man
Who could race like a god, bear the face of a god,
    whom a god loved so well;
He saw the land saved he had helped to save, and was
    suffered to tell
Such tidings, yet never decline, but, gloriously as he
    began,
So to end gloriously—once to shout, thereafter be
    mute:
"Athens is saved!"—Pheidippides dies in the shout
    for his meed.

HALBERT AND HOB

HERE is a thing that happened. Like wild beasts
      whelped, for den,
In a wild part of North England, there lived once two
      wild men
Inhabiting one homestead, neither a hovel nor hut,
Time out of mind their birthright: father and son,
      these—but—
Such a son, such a father! Most wildness by degrees
Softens away: yet, last of their line, the wildest and
      worst were these.

Criminals, then? Why, no: they did not murder and
      rob;
But, give them a word, they returned a blow—old
      Halbert as young Hob:
Harsh and fierce of word, rough and savage of deed,
Hated or feared the more—who knows?—the genuine
      wild-beast breed.

Thus were they found by the few sparse folk of the
      countryside;
But how fared each with other? E'en beasts couch,
      hide by hide,
In a growling, grudged agreement: so, father and son
      aye curled

The closelier up in their den because the last of their
    kind in the world.

Still, beast irks beast on occasion. One Christmas
    night of snow,
Came father and son to words—such words! more
    cruel because the blow.
To crown each word was wanting, while taunt matched
    gibe, and curse
Competed with oath in wager, like pastime in hell,—
    nay, worse:
For pastime turned to earnest, as up there sprang at
    last
The son at the throat of the father, seized him and
    held him fast.

"Out of this house you go!" (there followed a hideous
    oath)—
"This oven where now we bake, too hot to hold us
    both!
If there 's snow outside, there 's coolness: out with
    you, bide a spell
In the drift and save the sexton the charge of a parish
    shell!"

Now, the old trunk was tough, was solid as stump of
    oak
Untouched at the core by a thousand years: much
    less had its seventy broke

One whipcord nerve in the muscly mass from neck to
    shoulder-blade
Of the mountainous man, whereon his child's rash
    hand like a feather weighed.

Nevertheless at once did the mammoth shut his eyes,
Drop chin to breast, drop hands to sides, stand stiff-
    ened—arms and thighs
All of a piece—struck mute, much as a sentry stands,
Patient to take the enemy's fire: his captain so com-
    mands.

Whereat the son's wrath flew to fury at such sheer
    scorn
Of his puny strength by the giant eld thus acting the
    babe new-born:
And "Neither will this turn serve!" yelled he. "Out
    with you! Trundle, log!
If you cannot tramp and trudge like a man, try all-
    fours like a dog!"

Still the old man stood mute. So, logwise,—down to
    floor
Pulled from his fireside place, dragged on from hearth
    to door,—
Was he pushed, a very log, staircase along, until
A certain turn in the steps was reached, a yard from
    the house-door-sill.

Then the father opened eyes—each spark of their rage
    extinct,—
Temples, late black, dead-blanched,—right-hand with
    left-hand linked,—
He faced his son submissive; when slow the accents
    came,
They were strangely mild though his son's rash hand
    on his neck lay all the same.

"Hob, on just such a night of a Christmas long ago,
For such a cause, with such a gesture, did I drag—
    so—
My father down thus far: but, softening here, I
    heard
A voice in my heart, and stopped: you wait for an
    outer word,

"For your own sake, not mine, soften you too! Untrod
Leave this last step we reach, nor brave the finger of
    God!
I dared not pass its lifting: I did well. I nor blame
Nor praise you. I stopped here: and, Hob, do you
    the same!"

Straightway the son relaxed his hold of the father's
    throat.
They mounted, side by side, to the room again: no
    note

Took either of each, no sign made each to either: last
As first, in absolute silence, their Christmas-night
    they passed.

At dawn, the father sate on, dead, in the selfsame
    place,
With an outburst blackening still the old bad fighting-
    face:
But the son crouched all a-tremble like any lamb
    new-yeaned.

When he went to the burial, some one's staff he bor-
    rowed,—tottered and leaned.
But his lips were loose, not locked,—kept muttering,
    mumbling. "There!
At his cursing and swearing!" the youngsters cried:
    but the elders thought "In prayer."
A boy threw stones: he picked them up and stored
    them in his vest.

So tottered, muttered, mumbled he, till he died, per-
    haps found rest.
"Is there a reason in nature for these hard hearts?"
    O Lear,
That a reason out of nature must turn them soft
    seems clear!

EPILOGUE

ASOLANDO

At the midnight in the silence of the sleep-time
  When you set your fancies free,
Will they pass to where—by death, fools think, im-
      prisoned—
Low he lies who once so loved you, whom you loved
    so,
        —Pity me?

Oh to love so, be so loved, yet so mistaken!
  What had I on earth to do
With the slothful, with the mawkish, the unmanly?
Like the aimless, helpless, hopeless, did I drivel
      —Being—who?

One who never turned his back but marched breast
    forward,
  Never doubted clouds would break,
Never dreamed, though right were worsted, wrong
    would triumph,
Held we fall to rise, are baffled to fight better,
      Sleep to wake.

No, at noonday in the bustle of man's work-time
  Greet the unseen with a cheer!
Bid him forward, breast and back as either should be,
"Strive and thrive!" cry "Speed,—fight on. fare ever
      There as here!"